Published by Steve Allansc

First Printing, 2024

ISBN 978-1-3999-9346-3

I0090070

Images:

To my beautiful wife Ann who, for nearly fifty years, has encouraged
and supported me in every endeavour.

Aldar

A Puffin's Tale

A book by Steve Allanson

Including illustrations by Tracy Barnett and photographs by the author

1

Introduction

Aldar the Puffin

Mention the puffin to almost any European adult and most older children, and you can immediately sense that they are smiling within as they picture this gentle clown of the seabird world. But we should not be fooled into thinking this well-adapted, highly specialised ocean resident is a joke. It overcomes huge levels of adversity to successfully raise a single chick each year and to survive from year to year.

Its proper name is Fratercula arctica, meaning "northern friar" or "brother" a reference to the similarity to monks of its black and white garb. I'm not sure, though, how many religious orders would relish their adherents sporting the colourful outfit of the Atlantic puffin in full breeding attire.

In this phase, it sports bright orange legs, often the first thing to be seen when looking for puffins in a cliff setting. It also has a multi-coloured beak with vertical stripes of red, grey and orange, and with yellow and orange lines separating the beak from the face. At the corners of the beak are rosettes of bright yellow, which help it to hold many fish in its beak when bringing food back for the chick. The two parts of the beak itself are hinged so that they can open, to a degree, in parallel, again an adaptation to help the bird carry more fish such as sand eels or sprats, which they hold in a tidy line with the help of projections on the inside of their top jaw, called denticles, and with a strong tongue.

Its face, in breeding colour, is almost pure white with just a little fading to grey on the lower cheeks and a single grey stripe stretching back from each eye, as neat as any young lady could enhance her eyes with eyeliner. The eyes themselves are round but bordered with orange triangular growths and with additional grey elements on top of the triangle and along its bottom. Sometimes it is possible to glimpse the whites of the eyes, something quite rare in birds' eyes. The vast majority of people know what an Atlantic puffin is and could recognise a photograph or painting instantly, and yet most know very little of the life of this iconic and endearing seabird.

The puffin is usually seen in only one of its personae, that of the breeding adult described above. The young (the puffling) stays deep inside the burrow almost completely until it emerges ready to fly, only emerging very occasionally close to fledging at dusk and closely guarded by an adult. Indeed, pufflings have a strong aversion to light and will studiously avoid even being close to the entrance of the burrow in daylight.

Puffin with sand eels, Inner Farne, UK

The juveniles and wintering adults are seldom seen as they spend all their time out at sea in the Atlantic, and even if seen from a ship or boat, they are rarely recognised for what they are or are photographed. In both phases, the bird is much less colourful, with grey cheeks and, in the puffling, a much narrower beak which is almost totally grey. Over the next few years, the juveniles gradually gain some dull colouring and some of the vertical ridges associated with adults, but the bright coloured adornments are reserved for the breeding season. Adults out of season shed the very colourful plates on the beak and the legs as well as the bright eye markings. This is thought to be an adaptation to preserve energy and resources, as the breeding colours, which are derived from carotenoids from prey, require a high level of resources to produce and maintain. With such a high resource requirement, it makes evolutionary sense to only sustain the colours when needed for breeding display.

Carry out a web search for "juvenile puffin" or "puffin in non-breeding plumage" and you will discover that relatively few images appear. Ask one of the current manifestations of AI image tools to create a photo or painting of a juvenile or a puffin in non-breeding plumage, and the only thing that seems to register is the word "puffin", so that they produce the familiar multi-coloured face, bright beak and orange legs so familiar to visitors to Atlantic and North Sea cliffs in late spring and early summer.

The puffin has a comical marching walk.

In the UK, breeding colonies of puffins can be found at Flamborough in North Yorkshire, on the Farne Islands and Coquet Island in Northumberland, Skomer Island and South Stack Lighthouse in Wales, and the Isle of May along with the Shetland Islands and the Orkney Islands in Scotland. They are also present, in smaller numbers, on other similarly rugged coasts of the UK.

Female puffins lay a single egg each year, and this is incubated for between thirty-nine and forty-four days before the young chick hatches. The puffling takes between thirty-four and fifty days to be ready to fledge, the precise time taken being dependent mainly on the availability of fish, with most taking between thirty-eight and forty-four days. Once ready for fledging, they will emerge from the burrow at night to make a leap of faith from the cliff to the sea below. By the time the early morning light stretches across the sky, they will be far out on the sea, having instinctively paddled and flown away from land. Puffin parents do not usually stay with the chick once it fledges and, indeed, sometimes will continue to bring food to the burrow entrance for several days, only stopping and leaving the colony themselves once they realise the food is continually left uneaten at the burrow entrance.

In this book, we will explore more about this charming and comical seabird, both through further information on its natural history and through the life of Aldar, an imaginary puffin and the hero of our story. In the tale of Aldar, I have woven in some details of life, such as teaching the young to fish or each bird being named, which serve purely to enhance the fictional narrative. I hope the reader will forgive my straying, in an endeavour to create a more captivating narrative, into the realm of fantasy on those few occasions.

2

Aldar

Aldar emerges

It has been forty days since Aldar chipped and pushed his way out of his egg.

His doting parents have brought him regular meals of delicious small fish each day, starting with approximately four or five visits per day but increasing to an exhausting dozen or more by the time he was four weeks old. In the last few days, it has been noticeable that the number of visits has begun to decrease, and he has definitely lost some weight of late. His parents have also begun to leave the food at the entrance to the burrow rather than bring it directly to him, forcing him to venture from the deepest, darkest part of his home, where he has felt safest. His aversion to light is still extremely strong, and it is only with great determination that he has been able to bring himself to leave the earthy gloom and approach the entrance, but the smell of the fish is a great inducement for a hungry puffling.

In the last few days, the regular deliveries of food have declined even further, and hunger gnaws at his stomach. He can see, though, that it is still light outside, so he does not dare to emerge just yet, his father having warned him repeatedly of the marauding hunters outside the burrow. He knows he should not come out until it is completely dark and until he is ready to quickly make the leap into the cool night air and escape to the relative safety of the sea. Every additional second spent outside the burrow and on land increases the chances that a predator will find him and make a tasty snack of him.

For days now, he's been carefully preening and, for weeks, has been vigorously exercising his short but increasingly strong wings. He is apprehensive but confident, reasonably sure he can fly; however, he won't know with certainty until he launches from the cliff and opens his wings.

As the afternoon fades into the golden light of early evening, Aldar decides that this is to be the night he leaves the nest. He spends the next few hours on last-minute exercises and preening. He knows that his first tentative flight won't be a long one and that, unless he fails and plummets to an early and untimely death on the rocks, he will land on the water, so his newly grown juvenile feathers will need to be well waterproofed. Gone completely is the fluffy down that kept him warm in his first few weeks of life; he now has a coat of sleek, glossy black and grey feathers. Of course, he doesn't have the colourful beak of his parents, nor the clean white face and bright orange legs, but he knows these will come in time - if he survives his first few years.

The light at the opening of the burrow has now faded to a dull and barely perceptible grey; Aldar knows this means it must be full night out in the open beyond the warm, safe, earthy richness of the small and enclosed world where he has spent the first few weeks of his life. With slow and tremulous steps, he makes his way to the entrance and, even then, only after several minutes of mental preparation does he very tentatively poke his head outside. He has been fully outside the burrow only once, and that was with the reassuring presence of his father. This is a venture of an entirely different magnitude, so his nerves jangle and he is acutely aware of every scent and sound in the night air. He knows, though, that if he is to avoid starvation, he must take these final few steps into the unknown, step away from the comforting shelter of the burrow and try out his wings.

Listening carefully for the sounds of any potential enemies in the sky or hunting mammals on the ground, he edges just a little further out. He neither hears nor smells anything threatening, so, taking just one more moment to carefully look all around and appraise his surroundings with his already extremely well-adapted night vision, he ventures into the wide-open world alone. The mix of rock and soil just centimetres above his head is instantly replaced by the huge dome of deep black sky, pierced with a billion sparks of bright white light. The soundless, movement-free air of the burrow, with its dense mix of scents of fish, excrement and himself, is swept away by a brisk breeze, and he is assaulted by a seemingly endless array of new smells and noise. A cacophony of new sounds invades his ears: the hiss of the breeze through the grass, the mournful cry of the gulls, the growling of fellow puffins, and the echoing song of the kittiwakes. Behind it all is the constant booming and sibilation of the waves pounding the rocks below. For the briefest moment, Aldar feels an overwhelming urge to retreat into the familiar darkness of the burrow behind him. The world seems so terrifyingly full of a dizzying variety of new sensations and, at the same time, so wide and devoid of walls and ceiling. Then he sees the sea below him and, beyond the breakers, the heaving movement of the mountains and valleys of the water, the waves flecked with white flashes of foam as the wind tears at their tops rolling always towards the land. His fear turns to a deep sense of both belonging and adventure.

Aldar contemplates the leap from the cliffs.

Looking more closely around him, he sees that the clifftop is covered with a deep layer of soil covered with lush grass and a few summer flowers, such as pale pink thrift and the brighter red sea campion. There are also numerous other burrows, and Aldar can see that each one is guarded by one or two adult puffins, each nodding their colourful heads or stamping with their bright orange legs and webbed feet. He hears again the constant growling noises of puffin chatter against the louder cacophony of gulls and kittiwakes, "Kitt-i-waaaaaaake, Kitti-waaaaake." The smell of the colony is also very distinctive, a mix of fishiness and biting ammonia. Aldar will remember this until he returns to find or make a burrow of his own with his own mate. All around him, the cliffs pulse with life, and the air is filled with the general clamour that characterises a seabird colony in breeding season.

All of this has taken mere seconds, and now he looks again at the constantly moving sea below him and the waves breaking on the rocks. The moon has just risen above the horizon, and its baleful light bathes the sea in pale white light. Each wave below catches the light, throwing shards of reflected brightness into the small inlet below Aldar's narrow ledge.

The pull of the ocean below is becoming irresistible, and, coupled with the ever-present fear of predators, this drives the newly emerged puffling to take the few small steps that bring him to the edge. He spreads his sturdy wings, and, with a final short burst of flapping, he lowers his head and plunges into the void.

He immediately begins to plummet towards the deadly rocks below, finding that he must work his wings much harder than he imagined to provide any bite at all against the air. Flapping furiously, he finally begins to arrest the downward rush and feels the direction of his fall change by desperately slow degrees away from the vertical, moving him centimetre by centimetre away from the cliff and altering his trajectory beyond the rocks and out into the safety of the open water. He can see by the pale white light of the moon that the water below is filled with a stream of waves driving onto the rocks in a tumult of white spray and noise. He must get beyond that area and over the calmer, deeper waters before he attempts to land.

Only after a gargantuan effort and what seems like longer than the whole of his short life does Aldar see that he is at last over relatively clear water. He has made his first flight, albeit one that was only a fraction removed from a vertical plunge, but it is enough, barely, and he now belly-flops inelegantly into the sea and finds he bobs straight back to the surface and floats easily, rising and falling with the motion of the waves. He engages his strong legs and, paddling effectively with his webbed feet, makes rapid progress away from the cliffs and the dangerous spume and froth of the breakers. Within seconds, he accepts the constant motion of the water beneath him and, without thinking, sways his body with each wave, bending his neck to keep his head upright. This is his real home; the rigidity and non-moving nature of land will be alien to him for several years.

After only a short time, he finds himself surrounded by other puffins, both newly fledged like himself and adults. There are also numerous other types of seabirds, species he will come to know as guillemots and razorbills, black-headed and herring gulls. He is wary of these others but more so of any shadows above; he knows these could mean the larger gulls or birds of prey that would regard him as a tasty meal. The sea is a much safer place than land for a puffin, but even here, danger is something he must now live with. Aldar's life from now on will be a constant challenge, not only to feed himself but to learn about and avoid all the other threats to his life. He feels a pang of loss for the safety of the dark, musty burrow and its walls of solid and reassuring earth. Soon he must attempt to free himself again from the constantly moving surface of the ocean and master the ability to carry his body through the atmosphere, but before even considering that, he must find food to still the ravening hunger he feels.

Immediately at home on the water, Aldar paddled amongst his companions with his powerful webbed feet. Aware of the more experienced adult puffins around him, he decided to watch what they were doing, eager to learn the skills needed for survival. Aldar could see other newly fledged juveniles like himself all around him, but there were also adults in full breeding colours; clearly, these would be the ones to watch most closely.

He edged closer to one adult and, adopting a passive, non-threatening posture, let it be known that the other was his superior. The adult made a brief show of dominance - more for form's sake, Aldar thought; he was clearly no threat to the more experienced and larger male. They both sat quietly for some time, riding the swell of the ever-active ocean, but Aldar was hungry and was hoping his companion would show him how to find food. There was no possibility, of course, that the adult would feed him, and instinctively Aldar knew that he would need to dive to catch his own. He thought maybe he could just let instinct guide him, but there was no harm in taking a few lessons first if he could.

3

Hunting Lessons

Aldar's first dive. Original artwork by Tracy Barnett.

He soon got his wish, although he almost missed his chance as the adult gave little notice that he was about to dive. A quick flick of his tail, a powerful thrust with his feet at the same time as dipping his head beneath the surface and he was gone. Aldar did the same and was not far behind, watching closely. It was hard work keeping up as the adult made rapid and hard to predict changes of direction in all three dimensions – up, down, left or right; Aldar discovered that his wings were perfectly adapted to this new experience of underwater flight. It was an inversion of the world on the other side of the break between air and water only the water was more supportive and easier to thrust against. Above he had to work to stay airborne and down here he had to do the reverse as his body was naturally buoyant and would float to the surface if he didn't "fly" down. His wings were also a large part of his directional abilities along with his feet which he used like a rudder, this was exhilarating.

Suddenly he saw a flash of silver which he recognised as similar to the fish he was used to being provided with, but these weren't dead and still like those instead these were darting in all directions, scattering like an explosion of shimmering glittering particles as they recognised the threat of the two Puffins. The adult expertly targeted several individuals in quick succession and caught them in his gaping beak. He was obviously feeding himself as he didn't collect them in the serrations of his upper pallet, beautifully evolved for stacking them for transportation. Instead, he simply swallowed each one whole. They stayed below the surface for several minutes but didn't dive deep as the fish were conveniently gathered only a few metres under the glistening air/water interface. Aldar stayed as close to the adult as he could, reinforcing by observation that which his instinct already told him. Returning to the life sustaining air side of the world he again made a subservient gesture to the adult, signalling his thanks for the lesson and at the same time asking to be allowed to continue to watch. Again, the other made a purely token gesture of dominance which Aldar took to mean "You're welcome" and "please do continue."

On the third dive Aldar felt confident enough to try for himself, although his by now growing hunger was probably more of a driver than confidence or good sense. He focused on one glittering fish and lunged at it only for it to rapidly (and easily) change direction and completely evade his open beak. Again and again, Aldar lunged and again and again the fish easily avoided being caught until eventually the exhausted Puffin was forced to return to the surface to breathe. He could have sworn his adult teacher was grinning at him as he emerged. He decided to swallow his pride (instead of a juicy fish) and watch the skilful adult for several more dives before trying again for himself.

An adult shows Aldar how it's done.

He soon realised that the adult's success came not from lunging at where a fish was in that moment, but rather by anticipating where it would be a fraction of a second into the future and smoothly placing his open beak into exactly that space. Even this, he could see, was not foolproof, but the adult seemed to catch the targeted fish at least a third of the time. He could also see that, in the microsecond before the final thrust, the adult paused fractionally to avoid sending pressure waves at the fish, which would cause it to take evasive action.

Deciding it was time to try again for himself, Aldar gathered his breath at the surface and, with a silent offering to the gods of satiation, he dove again. A few metres down, he could see a large group of sand eels, and he manoeuvred himself behind and to one side of them and picked out an individual. He followed his target for several seconds, observing it closely and entering into the rhythm of its motion. Finally, he could perceive in his mind where it was going to be fractionally into the future, and he swiftly positioned himself, opened his beak, and then snapped it shut… on empty water.

Inwardly cursing, Aldar tried again and again, each time coming within millimetres of catching the fish, until finally, after a dozen or more attempts, he felt his beak close, not on nothing this time, but on the firm flesh of his prey. He quickly used his tongue and serrated beak in an entirely instinctive move and felt the fish slide satisfyingly and juicily down his throat.

Returning to the surface, Aldar clicked his beak and waved his head, indicating his success to the adult who was still with him. The adult now made to stand more upright on the water and gaped his own beak and opened his wings, clearly indicating that lessons were over and that Aldar should be grateful. He then paddled his feet rapidly until he was almost running on the surface, at the same time flapping his wings rapidly to take to the air and fly above the surface just as apparently effortlessly as he had below. Aldar still had to master this, but for the present, he was satisfied to stay on the sea and attempt more fishing dives.

It took some considerable time, but eventually, all the while slowly improving his hit rate, Aldar was sated and, tucking his head along his back, he closed his eyes and let the gentle rolling of the waves lull him into a state of semi-aware sleep.

4

Puffin Flight

Puffin in flight, Flamborough UK

Puffins are, surprisingly to some, very able fliers and are quite at home in the air. They can flap their wings at speeds of up to six hundred beats per minute, although four hundred beats per minute is more typical. They can reach speeds of nearly ninety kilometres per hour and can maintain speeds of sixty to seventy kilometres per hour for long periods.

They normally maintain an altitude of about ten metres above the surface of the sea, although, of course, they need to climb higher than this to reach their clifftop nest sites. Take-off from the sea surface is achieved by a combined effort from legs (remember, puffin feet are webbed) and wings, the bird eventually skipping or running along the surface until sufficient speed is achieved to become airborne. This whole process, though, takes seconds, and when disturbed, puffins will very quickly escape by flying.

Puffin running on the surface to take off.

Take-off from the cliffs is simply a case of throwing themselves from the ledge; they will usually then lose considerable height before the power of their wings brings about horizontal flight. Landing is an entirely different matter and is often ungainly at best. At sea, they will slow and angle their wings and essentially stall before belly-flopping onto the water. Occasionally, even this relatively controlled landing is pre-empted as they crash into the top of a wave and tumble into the water. On land, the birds will again slow their flight, drop their legs, and angle the wings in an attempt at a controlled stall on landing. In favourable windy conditions, it is possible to observe puffins almost hovering as they bring down their airspeed and then land gracefully, or nearly so, in front of their burrow. In more difficult conditions, they will often fall forward on landing, picking themselves up and shaking body and head as if regaining their dignity.

5

Alone

Aldar found himself alone on the wide ocean.

Aldar stayed amongst the other puffins for some days, gradually improving his hunting technique until he could readily catch the forty or so small fish needed to satisfy his hunger each day. He still had to work a lot harder than the experienced adults around him, but at least, for now, he was not in danger of starvation. He had also discovered that if he dived deeper, he could, if he were in a relatively shallow part of the sea or over a reef, catch delicious crunchy crabs, shrimps, and other shellfish. He had even, just once, caught a larger fish, which he had had to bring to the surface to eat as he couldn't swallow it whole under the water.

All this time he had simply moved around by paddling with his webbed feet, but he knew that at some point he had to tackle the challenge of flying. He had watched adult birds take to the air, so he knew in principle how to do it. He had also continued to exercise his wings as he had in the burrow, so his confidence was high.

The sun rose on a day much like the others he had experienced since landing on the sea, but one with a stiff breeze and yet a calm sea. The breeze was blowing from the cliffs he could still see not too far away, and this prevented any significant waves from developing. The air was chill but dry and smelled of both sea and of the scents blown from the land - grass and soil but also the unmistakeable smell of concentrated bird guano.

Aldar decided this should be the day of his test flight. He didn't count the barely corrected fall from the clifftop burrow to the sea as flight; he knew he had been lucky on that occasion to avoid crashing into the rocks below and bringing an end to his short life. This time he would have to get airborne from the surface of the sea without gravity assisting him. Once he had satisfied his morning hunger with a couple of fish and a tasty young crab, he raised his body above the water with some vigorous paddling and warmed up his wing muscles by flapping with gradually increasing vigour. He felt the strength of the well-developed muscles and the resistance of the air as he beat on the downstroke; this was the power stroke, the one that would keep him both moving forward and airborne. Not for Aldar the smooth, effortless gliding of the gulls - he would need to beat his wings around four hundred times every minute to maintain flight.

After a considerable period of practice, he felt the time was right and so he turned and faced into the breeze, instinctively knowing that this would give him the best lift. He started paddling forward, this time exerting as much effort as he could through his feet, while at the same time he flapped and flapped striving for the wingbeat speed required to lift his plump little body clear of the water. He reached the point where he was almost running on the surface and he could feel his body beginning to overcome the force which had, up to now, kept him firmly attached to the ocean. He tried to lift his feet - and immediately belly-flopped back into the sea, rolling helplessly forward and plunging headfirst beneath the surface.

He quickly righted himself and shook his head and his wings, looking around to see how many were silently laughing at his loss of dignity. Despite feeling that he had made a fool of himself, he was surprised to find that all the others were simply going about their own business, completely oblivious to the herculean effort he had just put into the attempt at flight.

Aldar knew, from watching others, that few succeeded at their first attempt and that even experienced adults sometimes failed to get airborne if the wind suddenly shifted or an unexpected wave brought their take-off run to an inelegant end. He gathered himself together for a few moments and set off again, this time deliberately bringing the attempt to an end just before the final push for flight and settling back on the water in a more controlled way.

He repeated this several more times, each time feeling he was nearer and nearer to the point where he could lift his feet to hang behind him in flying position. He was reaching the point where he knew he would need to rest and feed again when, completely unexpectedly, in those final few seconds before he settled again onto the grey-green sea, the wind gusted particularly strongly and, instinctively and without thought, flapping his wings harder to correct for this, he found he had lifted a foot or more from the rippling sea beneath him.

Aldar gave an internal shout of triumph and pushed his wings to flap even faster. He was airborne; he had conquered the attachment to the solid and liquid surfaces of the world and was now in a new three-dimensional world very similar to that beneath the waves.

He was Airborne!

He lifted a few more metres more from the sea and increased his speed before using his wings and feet, in the same way as he did in the undersea world, to turn away from the cliffs and out to sea. Had he known of speeds as measured by human beings, he would have recognised that he was now flying at more than eighty kilometres per hour, but this wasn't something he gave a thought to, being more interested in observing the raft of puffins below him as he flew over them and out over the clear sea.

Revelling in the feeling of freedom and exhilaration that flight brought, he continued on for nearly an hour as the morning slipped away. This was as much his world as the undersea one. He knew that, with time and maturity, he would be able to fly for hours at a time, skimming the waves and riding the wind on long journeys. He maintained a height of around eight or nine metres above the waves, but sometimes, for the sheer joy of it, he would dip down and almost touch the wave tops before lifting himself again. He practised some rapid turning manoeuvres, avoiding imaginary obstacles or predatory lunges, and sometimes just flew on in a straight line, exhilarated by this feeling of freedom.

Finally, he felt the pangs of hunger growing and, although not really tired, he began to look out for signs that there might be food below. Once he had spotted the unmistakable signs of fish, he decided to land and feed. Flying low towards the surface of the water, he lowered his airspeed and, abruptly braking sharply by changing his wing motion to push directly backwards against the direction of his flight, he dropped sharply onto the sea and, folding his wings, returned to the all-too-familiar paddling motion.

Before diving to search for the fish he knew were somewhere below him, he looked around. For the first time in his life, he could neither hear, see, nor smell another of his kind. Unconcerned, he set about finding food. He would spend the vast majority of the next four or five years alone on the vast ocean. This huge and largely empty world was his to explore, experience, and hopefully survive.

Aldar was alone; now he had truly fledged.

6

Puffins in Winter

Juvenile puffins, as well as adults, spend the winter alone on the ocean.

In winter, all Atlantic puffins migrate away from the colonies and range widely in the North Atlantic Ocean, rarely if ever coming to land. They bob about on the surface like bird-shaped corks and can survive cold and wet weather with little trouble. However, they can be badly affected by storms, either through drowning if caught in the wash of breaking waves or, more commonly, through the inability to feed in the disturbed top layers of the sea. Storms can also cause prey fish to migrate to greater depths, out of reach of puffins, who can only dive to around sixty metres and can stay underwater for only one or two minutes.

Storms kill thousands of puffins each winter and may well be one of the most significant causes of attrition of puffin populations from one breeding season to the next. When the dead birds are washed ashore in places such as Iceland, the Faroe Islands or Canada, they are known as "wrecks". As climate change adds energy to the atmosphere, this drives more frequent and more severe storms - just one of the challenges this human-induced catastrophe brings to puffins as well as other species.

7

Storm and Hunger

The North Sea in a storm.

It had been some weeks since Aldar flew out to sea and found himself alone for the first time. Since then, he had continued to improve his fishing skills and had mastered catching and eating larger fish. He had grown plump, strong, independent, and was gaining confidence both on the water and in the air.

Out there, he had seen few other puffins, indeed few other seabirds at all, but he was content to live alone on the wide ocean. Each day brought new curiosities and things to learn, along with, of course, new challenges. He still remembered the day he saw a great grey shape looming toward him on the sea, with its loud, rumbling engines that disturbed everything above and below the waterline. The only creatures that seemed not to fear it were the gulls, which Aldar had seen following the ship with their raucous calls. Aldar guessed they were looking for food, but instinctively he knew the ship was dangerous, so he moved away. This was one of the few occasions he felt the need to take to the wing, other than to practise flying. One day, he would have a much closer encounter with one of these monsters, but that was another story.

He had seen windy days and calm days, days of incessant rain (which didn't bother him in the least as his well-oiled feathers threw off even the heaviest of rain), and days of sun. Then, after many days at sea, there came a day that felt different. There was an electric, metallic smell in the air, and the sky was inky black in the west, even though Aldar knew it was the midpoint of the day, normally a time when the light was bright and full.

The sea was dead calm, with only the wide rolling of low, flat waves, and there was barely a whisper of breeze. Aldar sensed that something new was about to happen. He felt nervous and kept looking around, above, and below for predators. He was sure the strange weather meant danger.

Despite all of this, though, he had come across an area rich in fish and, throwing off the sense of imminent danger, continued to dive and feed. He still felt exhilarated when chasing prey, darting and weaving in the water, and those final moments when he linked with the movement pattern of the target fish, anticipating its next move. When he got this right, the feeling of his beak closing on firm, fishy flesh and the salty, meaty taste still gave him huge pleasure, but almost the pleasure of the hunt was even greater than the catch.

Each time he returned to the surface, the sky was darker, and the blackness in the west was closer and closer. The surface of the sea remained calm and glassy, but there were now hints of a breeze coming from the west. The situation was developing rapidly; after one more dive, Aldar returned to the surface to find it beginning to be disturbed by ripples and waves. The black clouds were only a few kilometres away, and he could see a wall of rain at the leading edge. He took a few moments to preen, renewing the oily coating on his feathers and tucking them into place, then he sat on the sea, faced into the wind, and waited.

Very quickly, the pounding rain arrived, and with it, an increase in the wind. The water was now covered in froth at the edges of small breaking waves, and Aldar thought that this was just the beginning.

Within a very short time - the time taken to make about ten dives—the conditions had deteriorated dramatically. Aldar was now rising and falling fifteen metres or more with the swell, and the wind constantly threatened to blow him over. Realising that this level of wind could easily damage more than just feathers, he tucked his wings tightly against his body and kept his head low. He continued to try to face into the main force of the wind; unfortunately, it changed often and rapidly, bringing random damaging waves on top of the ongoing swell from every direction. He was being buffeted more fiercely than he had ever known.

Suddenly, a large wave broke right in front of him, and Aldar was tumbled over and over in the driving white froth. This was very dangerous; Aldar was an excellent swimmer, but he was now completely at the mercy of the roiling force of the wave. On and on he rolled, unable to right himself or return to the surface. He could stay underwater for many minutes, but he was unprepared for this sudden and violent submersion, and for several seconds he didn't know what to do. Finally, he realised that he was being swept along with the charging wavefront and had to escape or die. He summoned all his strength and, rather than trying to reach the surface, he swam down. Deeper and deeper he forced himself until he could feel a lessening of the wave's hold. He was no longer spiralling out of control, and the water down there was less dangerous.

Aldar overwhelmed. Original artwork by Tracy Barnett.

But Aldar was not a fish, and he knew he would need to return to the surface soon. He could see the continuing savage turbulence above and tried to spot a patch of relative calm where he could break through. He knew he had to avoid the areas of white chaos and looked for a large enough expanse of darker water. Choosing one, he swam rapidly upwards and broke the surface on the rear side of a large swell. At first, he plunged rapidly with the water, then rose just as quickly with the next wave until he crested twenty metres above the oncoming trough. He had survived, but only barely, and he knew he was going to be battling for his life for many hours to come.

The wind howled demonically around him, and the sea had been whipped into a frenzy of froth and spume. The air was filled with the noise of the wind and the drumming of the rain on the water. Aldar could not relax for a second; he needed to anticipate every movement of the ocean, keep his body as small and tightly packed as he could, and watch for any oncoming walls of white violence.

Several more times he was caught by these and swept uncontrollably under the surface, but he was at least now slightly better prepared to swim down as soon as possible to escape the torrent, returning to the surface only when he found an area of darkness. On one such return, he was unfortunate enough to be immediately engulfed in yet another newly formed breaker, with barely enough breath left to escape once again and break the surface. Had this happened a third time, he suspected that would have been the end.

The storm seemed to rage on interminably, and Aldar was nearing exhaustion. Never in his short life had his body felt so battered and so close to collapse. He had no idea where he was, having been swept along with the storm for many kilometres, and all his normal guidance senses were utterly overwhelmed.

After what felt like an eternity, he noticed a slight but discernible lessening of the assault, but the poor battered puffin knew he was not yet completely safe. He dug deep into his last reserves of strength and fought on.

Many hours later, the storm had died away, and Aldar sat, exhausted and drained, on the surface. He needed to eat but barely had the strength to dive. In one final push, he dove beneath the surface. Below, the sea was entirely empty—a boundless volume of water, an endless grey-green void. There were no fish! They had all escaped the storm by swimming deeper than Aldar, in his weakened state, could reach, or they had scattered so widely that the chances of finding a meal in the endless ocean seemed slim.

Returning to the surface, Aldar tucked his head into his feathers, closed his eyes, and surrendered to unconsciousness.

8
Hunger

After the storm.

Aldar opened his eyes on a seascape very different to the one he had lived through just a few hours earlier. The sky was a vivid pale blue, etched with long trails of wispy white clouds that appeared to be stretched by the wind, which was still blowing stiffly out of the west.

He tentatively extended his wings and legs, noting the stiffness but no discernible damage. His primary sensation was of an empty belly and ravenous hunger, and he remembered how he had tried, without success, to find food after the storm. Giving his body a final shake, he dived under the water and set about the search for small fish. After several minutes, he returned, unsuccessful and still hungry, to the surface. Concluding that this area was not going to provide him with anything to eat, he took to the wing and flew west, towards the shore he had originally launched from many weeks ago. He hoped that nearer the shore, in shallower water, he would find food.

For the rest of the day, he searched along a route to the west, looking from the sky for the telltale signs of fish and often stopping and diving to search. But by nightfall, he was still hungry; he had managed to catch one solitary medium-sized fish, which he had gladly devoured on the surface. This was nowhere near enough to sustain him, though, so he continued the search through the night.

Another new day broke with a watery, pale grey sky, and Aldar once again launched himself into the air and flew on westwards.

After an hour or so of flying against the wind, he saw several birds, including one or two puffins, on the sea and apparently feeding. Joining the group at the edge, he immediately dived and was relieved to find fish in relative abundance. Aldar gratefully gorged himself on as many as he could catch, but without feeling the usual enjoyment of the chase. At this time, he was solely focused on assuaging his intense, all-consuming hunger. At last, when he could eat no more, he settled on the surface, faced into the wind, and slept again.

Waking once again after a few hours, he was immediately aware that the sky was now a deeper, steely grey and the wind was freshening briskly. The sea was already more disturbed, and whitecaps were beginning to form again on the tops of the racing waves. Clearly, another storm was coming.

Aldar dived repeatedly, again and again, once more bingeing on the fish that were still available in this part of the sea. Something told him he needed to stay a little nearer to land this time and that this would, hopefully, provide some respite from the ferocity of the coming storm. But he also knew, instinctively, that being too close to shore put him in danger of being washed or blown onto the rocky coast, with potentially catastrophic results. The small gathering of birds that had drawn him to this spot had dispersed, although he could still vaguely discern a few in the distance. Aldar knew that gathering in numbers offered no protection at all from the weather and that he was alone again in his struggle for survival.

He fed several more times during the day and preened often to prepare for the coming ordeal. The clear memory of the last storm remained with him, and he knew that each of these new experiences gave him new skills valuable to a long-lived bird such as a puffin, as long as he survived them. Late in the day, the storm hit with somewhat less ferocity than the last, but nevertheless, Aldar had to struggle his way through an exhausting night and well into the next morning - a morning that broke with little brightening of the sky and a continued battering of his little body. By late morning, the storm had passed, and the sky showed glimmers of blue through the still thick cloud cover. Once more, he set out to find life-sustaining food beneath the waves, but as before, he found that the storm had driven the fish into the deeper areas of the ocean - areas he could not reach. He had no choice but to take to the air again in search of fish.

For what seemed like an eternal succession of days, Aldar battled his way through storm after storm, with only brief periods of time in between - respites that were barely long enough for Aldar to find food and feed sufficiently to survive the next tempest. He knew he was gradually weakening, never getting enough food between the bouts of bad weather to quite return to the peak of condition with which he had entered the first, and, so far, most tumultuous storm. Much more like this, and he would join the dead seabirds he had begun to see floating on the surface of the sea. The sad, bedraggled bodies of both adults and juveniles like himself were testament to a succession of violent and unrelenting outbursts.

Fortune, though, was with him, and for several weeks after one last battering, the skies remained clear, and the storms ceased. The temperatures were much lower now, and the wind very rarely dropped altogether, but none of these things bothered Aldar. Indeed, he now knew he could, with luck and strength, survive the storms themselves. The much more difficult problem was that each storm both scattered and drove deeper the fish that Aldar needed to rebuild his resources and continue to survive.

From somewhere deep within his species memory rose the thought that he could find somewhere with a greater abundance of food and less severe storms. As time passed, and the weather remained cold and windy but stormless, the shoals of sandeel and sprat regathered close to the surface, and Aldar was able to enjoy several days of good feeding. He felt that most of his condition had returned. His bruises had healed, and he had regained some of the coating of fat from a diet rich in high-calorie oily fish. He was still not the plump bird who had flown away from the shore for the first time in summer, but he was tougher, more experienced, and stronger.

The time had come to follow the instinct to head for somewhere else, to continue his youthful explorations of the ocean world. Aldar shook himself, stood on the water and flapped his wings, ran along the surface, and launched himself once again into the world of air.

He turned and headed south.

9

Juvenile Puffin Travels

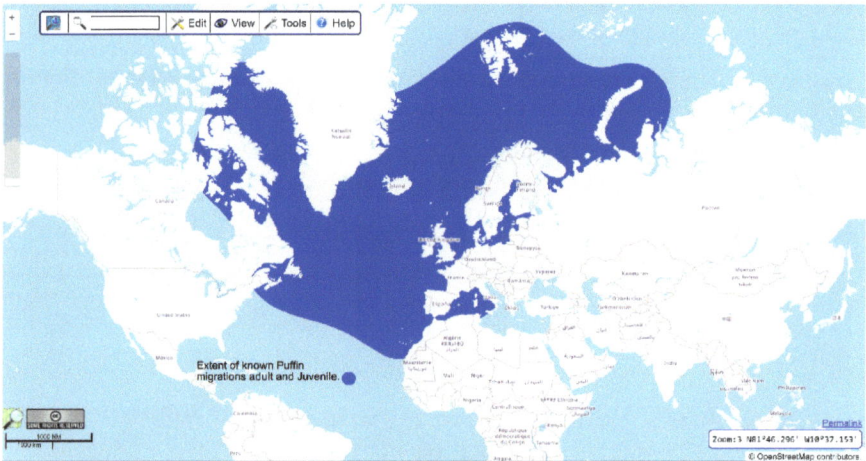

Map showing extent of Atlantic Puffin Migrations - created using
Openseamap.org under Creative Commons Licence
https://creativecommons.org/licenses/by-sa/2.0/

Adult puffins migrate far from the breeding colony in the winter, and it is known that the routes they take are highly individual but repeated each year. It is likely that these are not genetically determined but "learned" by young puffins in their pre-breeding years of travel.

The young puffin will not return to the colony for around four years, during which time they range widely north, south, east, and west. Data from ringing studies have shown that puffins from the UK range over a vast area of the Atlantic Ocean, from Greenland and Canada in the west to Norway and Iceland in the north and east, and into the Mediterranean Sea as far east as Sicily. They are rarely, if ever, found inland, and to reach Italy they will have flown and paddled through the Straits of Gibraltar and on into the Mediterranean rather than overland.

The majority of UK-born puffins, though, will range, both on their youthful exploratory voyages and eventually on their winter migrations, from the Bay of Biscay in the south to Iceland in the north and out into the mid-Atlantic in the west.

Both their juvenile journeying and their winter migrations are solitary, although they will encounter other birds. Specifically, although they mate for life, they do not spend winter with their partners, meeting up again only back at the colony in late spring.

10

South

Aldar goes south.

Immediately after Aldar took to the air, he felt an urgency to be away from the area where he had so nearly perished. He flew as if being pursued by one of the dark black storm centres, wings beating frantically, skimming the waves beneath him. He soon realised, though, that he wouldn't be able to keep this up for a long flight, so he deliberately slowed his pace, bringing his wingbeat rhythm down to a more sustainable level and pushing away the fear of storms that had been threatening to rise in him. He flew south for many hours, keeping the distant coast always to his right. The weather, thankfully, remained cold but relatively calm and clear, with the wind from the east or northeast giving a little assistance to the young puffin.

He had seen many small and larger boats on the water but, still wary of the unknown, he avoided them and would adjust his flight to stay a good distance away as he passed them. Each vessel was accompanied by loudly crying, wheeling groups of gulls that would drop down into the water behind the boats, presumably to feed on something left behind. Aldar, though, wasn't interested in feeding from the scraps left by boats, preferring live, fresh fish and crustacea.

Anticipating a long journey, he landed often to hunt and could usually, for now, find sufficient prey to satisfy his hunger and power his flight from the storms. Sometimes he would simply paddle along on the surface of the sea, content in the calmer weather to make progress in this way. He rarely saw other puffins, and if he did happen upon one, they would perhaps give a nod or a shake of the head. There was no vocalisation, though; such encounters were always silent. He could remember the constant chatter of the colony, with the mooing and grunting of his fellow puffins accompanied by the calls of the nearby kittiwakes. But on the sea, even when encountering groups of puffins, Aldar, like all others of his kind, was entirely silent.

The sounds of Aldar's world were now the calls of other bird species, the howl of the wind, and the constant, all-pervading sound of the sea. Of course, there were also the alien, coarse, and disruptive sounds that emanated from anything to do with humans. Several times, as he moved south, Aldar had heard the deafening scream of something flying high and very fast far above him. He had learned not to panic when this happened, as no harm seemed to come to him, even though the noise hurt his ears and made him think the world was collapsing.

The noise of the passing tanker was terrifying.

As time passed and his journey continued, he came to a region where the ocean seemed to be getting ever more crowded with boats, large and small. Many made their way into the sea from wide openings in the coast, whilst others travelled either north or south, with just a few vessels, appearing to be full of human creatures, moving east to west or west to east. Some of the boats were huge, up to a thousand times his height, and took him many heartbeats to fly past. The smooth, steely sides rose above him like huge, perfectly smooth cliff faces. Each of these encounters was accompanied by an unnatural, bitter, chemical stench and a deep, throbbing, pulsating noise, intermittently pierced by harsh, clanging sounds.

At this point in the journey, the sea narrowed so that Aldar could see land on both sides, and this continued for some time. But once past this channel, the sea expanded again rapidly. With every passing day, the weather was calmer and the air - and indeed the sea - warmer. As he travelled yet further south, he saw land looming in front of him and, not yet satisfied that he had reached the limit of his migration, he turned west, remaining far from the shore but following its path, always pursuing the wide ocean which he was sure lay ahead.

Eventually, the landmass retreated again southwards as Aldar's flight brought him into a large, northward-facing bay with a few large islands located in its central region. Stopping here for a while, he found fish in abundance, so it was an easy decision to rest and feed, rebuilding his strength. There was a significant amount of disturbance from the movement of boats, large and small, between the larger islands, as well as smaller craft moving around haphazardly in the whole area. The fishing, though, was good, and so Aldar stayed in this vicinity for a while, always keeping well away from the islands. Even from far out to sea, he could hear the endless tumult of human existence and could see, at night, the flickering of their lights reflecting haphazardly on the rippling sea. He instinctively felt that human presence signified danger, something he would come to know for certain as he matured.

After some days, he continued southwest and then south again into a wide expanse of open sea. In the area near the shores to the east, the sea was often exceedingly rough, with waves bigger than any he had seen before. But at the moment, there were simply huge rolling waves moving regularly and in fairly straight lines out of the west. He wondered what storms would be like in this region and decided he wouldn't like to be trapped here if the regular wave pattern turned into the chaotic mess he had experienced further north. Moving further west, he came to a place where he sensed the ocean depth increased dramatically. He could feel the temperature change of the cold water welling up from the depths as the wind-driven current collided with the steep westward-facing underwater slopes. Here he was far from the humans and their noise and smell, and on clear nights, the sky was utterly black, and the stars shone with undimmed brilliance. The lights in the heavens always seemed to be dimmed by the scattered lights of the human creatures but shone with unsullied magnificence when these artificial illuminations were absent. The Milky Way arched brilliantly overhead, and when the moon shone, it did so with a clarity and beauty to take the breath away.

Aldar, of course, although he noticed these things, was not concerned with the exquisiteness of the moonlight but rather with the way it lit the undersea world and reflected from the scaly sandeel skin, rendering them easier to see and to hunt. Here the fish were present in copious abundance, the whole food web supported by nutrients in the upwelling water - plankton-feeding small fish and squid, which in turn fed Aldar.

When the first storm came sweeping out of the west, Aldar moved from the shallower waters into the deeper ocean, where the impact, although still severe, was less destructive than further east. Aldar found he could more easily ride out the peak of the crisis on the deeper water relatively unscathed. Although it was still harder to find food in the immediate aftermath of the storm, this seemed to the young puffin to be less pronounced than in the sea to the north. Maybe this was also due to him sustaining less damage than from the unpredictable breakers he had encountered earlier, or maybe he was just more experienced and better able to cope. Whatever the reason or reasons for his improved condition, in this way Aldar saw out his first winter - an important landmark in the life of a puffin and one which marked a transition from the period of greatest vulnerability to a part of his life that would be spent exploring his oceanic world and building his strength, experience, and expertise in readiness for when he would seek out a mate.

Aldar had passed from fledgling to juvenile.

11

Human Threats to Puffins
1 Netting

Gill nets are vast nets that are anchored to the sea bottom and left floating for many hours before subsequent retrieval; drift nets are similar but are not anchored. Both pose a risk to various mammal and seabird species, including Atlantic puffins. It is a sad fact that the areas important to human fishing are, of course, the same areas that are important to puffins and other birds, particularly in the breeding season.

Once caught in a net, a bird will almost certainly drown as it is held underwater. In the parlance of the fishing industry, this is known as "bycatch". The trapped birds are of no value to the fishermen and are simply discarded.

Thousands of puffins are routinely drowned by being caught in deployed fishing nets, particularly gill nets or drift nets.

12

Tangled

Between the almost invisible filaments were holes to trap and unwary puffin.

As the days started to get longer and temperatures increased, Aldar felt again the desire to explore the vast ocean that had become his abode. For several days, he had been paddling steadily north-westwards, drawn by some inner sense to move further into the Atlantic and, at the same time, to move back into the colder north. In time, the stocks of fish and tasty meals of small squid began to diminish, and so, instinct telling him that there were other areas further north where conditions would again favour the consolidation of food, he spread his wings and added flight to his onward journey. He did not return along the path he had taken in early winter but moved further out into the Atlantic, eventually travelling to the west of Ireland.

Aldar stayed away from the coast, not wanting to venture over land. In his mind, there were many reasons for this: there was, of course, no food on land, but there were also many more predators and many more humans. He remembered how his parents would pause at the entrance to the burrow and, on first emerging, would stand for a moment and scan both the air and the ground, looking for danger. They had instilled in him an innate fear of predators on land, one he would only put aside when the time came to raise his own chick each year. This summer was, of course, not one when Aldar would consider finding a mate. He was far too young for that yet and would spend several more years exploring, growing, and gaining the experience he would need to overcome the challenge of providing for a ravenous youngster before he was ready to become a parent.

The further north he travelled, the more productive the sea became, and so he gradually regained weight and condition after the rigours of winter. Life was a little easier now that summer was advancing, although he still had to be wary of predators, mainly from below when on the ocean. There were more days when the sky was an unblemished blue, and the gentle swell of the sea offered a pleasant and soothing platform on which a sated puffin could snooze away an hour or two until the urge to fish once again roused him. Even when resting on the water in such an apparently benign situation, though, Aldar would often put his head under the surface to scan for any dangers, which he knew might include sharks, large fish, orca, or seals. A puffin's place in the web of life was as both a hunter and a tasty morsel for larger carnivores.

The wide, grey-green sea was never still but, at this time of year, rarely would severe Atlantic storms move in to give Aldar cause for concern. It did, though, rain constantly; barely a day would go by without a period of, sometimes heavy, downpours. The deluges would sometimes beat down on the surface of the rolling ocean with a noise like thunder, seemingly flattening the waves themselves, but even in the heaviest inundation, the rain would run freely from his glossy, well-oiled plumage. He worked hard to keep it in good condition, spending time every day spreading oil from his preen gland and working each feather into place. Rarely would the rain cause him to pause in his hunting, as his eyes were very well adapted both to the underwater world and to the dark.

This was a time for Aldar to relish as well as further enhance his fishing skills. He had become extremely adept at seemingly entering the mind of his target prey, anticipating its movements so that he could strike at just the right moment. In those last critical seconds, it was almost as if he saw the watery world through the eyes of his prey and was so closely entangled with it that he simply knew where and when it would turn.

Continuing slowly north and somewhat east, he eventually came to a group of rugged islands off the east coast of a larger landmass. He could see that there were breeding colonies of puffins here on the islands, but he stayed well away and out at sea, only encountering the adult breeding birds as they came out to fish. Initially, these adults only fed themselves, but as the weeks passed, they were more frequently seen carrying beak-loads of fish back to the island colonies. Aldar fed on the same fish shoals as the adults and sometimes spent a little time in the rafts of birds that had gathered over a particularly large grouping of prey fish. It felt good to be amongst his own kind for short periods of time, although his solitary wanderings were in no way marred by feelings of loneliness. As with all puffins, Aldar was very comfortable with his own company.

Around these islands, he also noticed more of the boats of humans, and several times Aldar saw them hauling in huge catches of fish. On one otherwise ordinary day, there were several of the boats on the water, and puffins and other seabirds were also hunting. Aldar had had several successful dives but was not quite sated, so he dived again, with no thought of any danger beneath the surface beyond the usual concerns about predators.

Spotting a group of fish, he entered hunting mode, selected a target, and began to follow it, closely mimicking its movements this way and that. He was just about to pounce, using his powerful wings and feet to turn rapidly in anticipation of where the fish would be in the next moment, when he felt himself collide with something at his side. His wing on that side was suddenly brought to a complete stop, his passage through the water was abruptly arrested, and he was twisted violently to one side. The fish slipped away, and Aldar tried to make for the surface, only to find his wing was caught and was holding him under the water. Looking closely, he could see a shimmering wall - a web of fine filaments - which extended from the depths almost to the surface on that side of his body. Between the filaments were holes into which he had inadvertently pushed his wing. He pulled hard on the wing, but that merely brought the rest of his body, his other wing, and his feet into contact with the clearly dangerous object.

Aldar tried again to pull his wing free and put his foot against one of the filaments to help, but it slipped off and, in its turn, passed through one of the holes. By now, Aldar realised his danger and instantly pulled the leg back. He knew he must free himself so that he could return to the surface to breathe, and he fought to control the panic he could feel rising.

Instinctively, he twisted sharply in the water, turning away from the mesh, and was incredibly relieved to feel his caught wing come free. With a sense of deadly danger escaped, he turned for the surface and, in that moment, saw that the net had caught many fish. Their heads had passed through the holes, and they were now caught fast by their gills, unable to go forwards because the holes were not big enough to allow their bodies to pass, and unable to retreat as the filaments were caught behind their gills.

He momentarily considered trying to catch and eat one of these unfortunate fish to replace the one he had been about to catch when, to his horror, he saw that several puffins were also caught in the net. They had become hopelessly tangled in the web, and some had already drowned, their bodies now hanging limply in the water. Others were still struggling to escape but were rapidly running out of air. Their panicked struggles served only to entangle them even more until eventually they couldn't move at all. Aldar could both see and sense their desperation, but there was nothing he could do to assist them. He now realised what an incredibly lucky escape he'd had. If his wing had not come free so quickly, and if his leg had not pulled free so easily, he too would have been trapped. Although he could stay under the water for several minutes, he knew that, had he been caught more strongly, he would soon also have run out of air and would have perished and become one more limp and lifeless body hanging in the water.

With feelings of great sadness and revulsion, he swam rapidly to the surface, all the while trying to comprehend the net and why it was there. Once on the surface, he immediately made the connection with the human boats in the area. If he stayed here to fish, he would never know when a dive might result in him being caught in one of the nets. He turned from the scene and, running along the surface to gain speed, almost overcome by dread, he took to the air and flew away from both the fishing vessels and the islands, heading once again into the north and the open ocean.

Aldar had learned another valuable life lesson and had reinforced again the need to avoid these strange human creatures who made so much noise and seemed to care so little about the destruction their activities wreaked upon other species.

In the next few weeks, he would have an encounter that would leave him with even more cause to fear humans above all predators.

13

Whale

Aldar and the whale. Original artwork by Tracy Barnett.

Aldar had flown for many hours since his encounter with the deadly net in the sea, always heading north towards colder waters and emptier ocean. He had passed several of the human fishing vessels but had given them a very wide berth. What he didn't know was that, in fact, the nets were often set and simply left, so that the absence of a vessel was no guarantee that the sea was clear of them. What was true, though, was that as he moved into emptier waters in the vast reaches of the Atlantic, the chances of encountering nets or ships decreased.

In this part of Aldar's world, when there was no moon, the night sky was the deepest black, beyond anything he had ever seen. The vault would be filled with piercing white pinpricks of planets, stars, and galaxies - things that would never come within the comprehension of the growing puffin. He simply knew that there were lights in the sky which were reflected in the sea. On calm nights, it was sometimes impossible to see where the sea ended and the sky began. The water around Aldar lay like a great silk gown bejewelled with bright white diamonds, flowing seamlessly into the heavens above. He was cocooned in a great black, sparkling world.

More often, though, the ocean moved like a living thing, the long breaths of the swell overlaid with shorter, sharper waves and wind-driven ripples. The puffin was totally at home on the ocean, needing no effort to stay afloat even with the constant movement of the surface. Only severe storms and the unpredictable chaos of crashing, breaking waves driven by huge winds continued to cause him any noticeable disturbance. The sky and sea were his natural habitat - only land was alien to him, and he had no need of that for many seasons yet.

In time, the trauma of the dead and dying puffins caught in the net faded into just another experience, and he stopped being quite so wary every time he dived. He had, though, added a scan for the shimmer of the gillnet to his panoply of lookouts when entering the underwater world of prey. Aldar grew in skill as well as size and weight throughout the autumn. Instinctively, he increased his body fat in preparation for winter and the likelihood of more storm-driven periods of food scarcity. He was quite the sleek and healthy young puffin now, still in the predominantly grey and black juvenile plumage, but handsome nonetheless.

As his experience grew, he was also becoming more familiar with the creatures with which he shared the ocean. He had seen seals and orcas, dolphins and many other types of seabirds, and, of course, the huge variety of fish - some of which he viewed as food and some of which would in their turn view him as a tasty snack.

One moonlit night, Aldar was dozing on the surface, still partially alert for predators or human ships but only semi-conscious. He was snapped sharply into full wakefulness by the thunderous sound of rushing water. Instantly awake, he saw, no more than ten metres away, a great spout of sea rising into the night and shining brightly with reflected moonlight. At the same time, something rose out of the depths and broke the surface like a new island forming instantly in the sea. It continued to lie there, moving only slowly, and after deciding it didn't pose an immediate threat, Aldar swam closer. Only when he was right next to the creature did he realise it was alive: a great eye, almost as big as Aldar himself, broke the surface and stared straight at the tiny puffin. In an instant, a connection formed between the two creatures - not prey or predator, but fellow hunters of fish, fellow voyagers of the great oceans of the world.

They sat alongside each other for some time, the gigantic body of the humpback whale dwarfing the puffin, not communicating in any way we know but somehow connected, knowing that, despite the obvious differences, they had some level of shared experience in the ecosystem of the world. Aldar sensed a vastly older and wiser intellect was with him and that it regarded him with benevolent compassion and understanding.

Eventually, the whale began to move forward, leaving Aldar sitting in its wake on a disturbed sea. It ducked its head under the surface and lifted its great tail as if waving farewell to the seabird. In a few seconds, it was gone, leaving Aldar alone again on the gradually calming water. Somehow the ocean seemed even more vast and empty now that the creature had departed. The juvenile bird sat for some time pondering the encounter, then once more tucked his head onto his back, closed one eye, and slept.

The wandering puffin continued north for many more days - days spent paddling along the surface, diving to feed, and occasionally taking to the wing and flying short distances. Although the weather continued to get colder and there were several periods of rain, there were no major storms, so Aldar made steady progress without really having a specific destination in mind.

After some weeks of wandering, he sighted a distant island group with steep, rugged grey cliffs topped by green pastures. It was too late in the season now for there to be breeding adults on the shore, although Aldar had encountered a few individuals on the sea. He wondered vaguely if this would make a good alternative breeding place when the time was right, and so paddled closer to explore the coast. The wind had lately increased in strength, and the rolling North Atlantic waves crashed dramatically against the cliffs, raising ascending cascades of white spray which sometimes came close to overtopping the cliffs themselves. The salty spray then fell back to the water or blew along the cliffs, shrouding the islands in an enveloping mist.

Through the spume and spray, Aldar could see and hear wheeling gulls and other large seabirds. As a relatively mature bird, over a year old now, he wasn't the easy prey that a newly fledged bird presented but nevertheless, he wasn't going to land on shore and make an easier target. Here on the sea, he could always dive if threatened from above, but on land he did not have that option.

Looking around, he could see some human boats on the sea, but these didn't appear to be the large fishing vessels he now associated with the shimmering wall of death. So, he took advantage of what he thought would be a plentiful supply of fish and crustacea just offshore and settled into a feeding routine.

14

Human Threats to Puffins
2 Hunting

Today, most people would be appalled at the idea of taking large numbers of puffin eggs or shooting the birds, but we need only go back to the nineteenth century to find both practices were widespread. For example, large numbers of people would either gather on the clifftops of Flamborough or hire boats out of Bridlington and Scarborough with the sole intention of shooting as many seabirds as possible purely for "sport". Thousands of puffins were shot and left to rot in the sea each year until the practice was ended.

It was the Rector of The Priory Church in Bridlington, the Reverend H.F. Barnes-Lawrence, together with the East Yorkshire MP, Christopher Sykes, who, motivated to end what they saw as appalling and needless slaughter, introduced the Protection of Seabirds Bill to the House of Commons on twenty-sixth February 1869. This became law in June of that same year and made it illegal to shoot any seabird in the UK except on the island of St Kilda. In 1954, the Wild Birds Protection Act also made it illegal to collect the eggs not only of seabirds but of all wild birds in the UK.

In Norway, meanwhile, a special breed of dog, the puffin dog or Norwegian Lundehund, was bred to be able to go down into puffin burrows and drag out live puffins, which were then skinned, cooked, and eaten. Thankfully, puffin hunting is now illegal in Norway, although the dog breed still exists as a cuddly but playful family pet.

The hunting of puffins remains legal and is practised annually in Iceland and in the Faroe Islands. In both places, the primary method of capture is using aerial nets in the breeding season, but the birds are also shot from boats in the winter months.

15

Hunted

Aldar took no notice of the small boats.

Our juvenile puffin fed until sated and then sat on the rolling sea, looking again at the island immediately in front of him. Once more, he was struck by the towering, rugged cliffs and the lush green appearance of the land on top. He thought it looked like ideal territory for a breeding puffin to raise a chick. Instinct, though, was powerful, and instinct would eventually draw him back to the colony of his hatching, so he filed the thought away and set out to explore the group further, he could see there several other islands beyond this one.

As he paddled and flew around the islands, always careful to stay away from the shore, he saw they were inhabited by humans and their livestock. Again, he saw gulls and skuas, along with many of the other seabirds alongside which he had been raised back at the colony. In the sea, the fish, crabs, and other tasty prey were seemingly plentiful, and he had no trouble satisfying his hunger and indeed continued to improve his general condition.

In the southwest, the skies were darkening, first to a dull steel grey and then deeper to an almost inky black. Aldar now knew that this meant an incoming storm, and in general, the darker the sky as it approached, the more ferocious and potentially more damaging the tempest would be. Some instinct made him paddle into the sea between the largest of the islands and a group of smaller ones to the northeast, to sit out whatever the next few hours might bring.

The storm hit, and his world narrowed from wide horizons to a much smaller space bounded by curtains of torrential rain, the fat drops coming down with such ferocity that they bounced back from the sea, making it appear almost as if the sea was fighting back, trying to cast the waters back into the heavens from where they came.

Then the wind picked up and drove the deluge sideways so that Aldar, as he faced always into the wind, was pounded relentlessly from the front. The sea itself, although wilder than before the storm, did not generate the killing waves he had experienced a whole year ago in his first experience of such weather. He was rocked from side to side as the waves were swept around either side of the larger island and into the channel in which he sheltered. Even though they came from both sides, creating a chaos of collisions and rebounds, they remained relatively small compared to the giants out in the open ocean. There weren't the towering breakers here that could instantly cast the puffin under the surface and leave him struggling to return to air.

Nevertheless, the storm was an exhausting time for any small seabird; anyone watching would have seen our puffin bobbing around on the wild sea, struggling constantly to keep himself facing into the teeth of the gale despite the buffeting he was receiving from wind, wave, and rain.

For many hours, the storm raged on and, of course, one of the ongoing impacts was that Aldar was unable to feed as long as it did so. Once the sky cleared and the wind died down to a steadier force, it left him tired and hungry. Here again, the instinct that had driven him to shelter behind the larger island paid off. Here, where the devastation was somewhat reduced, the fish were less scattered and also less inclined to be driven to depths where a puffin could not reach them, and so Aldar was able to feed much sooner and regain his strength.

Increasingly, it seemed to Aldar that this might be a good place to see out the coming winter months with their more frequent storms and colder weather. How wrong he was. He had no idea of the much greater danger a wintering puffin in the Faroe Islands faced than that from even the worst winter convulsions on the open sea.

The ever-weakening wintry sun rose the next day into a sky washed clean by the recent blast, a sky gleaming a pale blue and dashed with streamers of high white cloud. The wind was still high, and the sea fitful with racing waves and the spume and froth that humans know as white horses. Our bird was to be found riding the waves and diving frequently into the depths, returning to breathe sometimes already having greedily snaffled his prey underwater and sometimes with a larger fish safely lodged in his beak, ready to feast on the surface.

He took no notice of the small craft rounding the island and entering the channel from the southeast. Each boat carried several humans, and Aldar assumed they would be fishing. As they advanced through the channel, he could hear faint pops or bangs from the vessels, but they were still too far away for Aldar to perceive any danger. He dived again, engaging his hunting skills to capture and devour several small fish before returning to the surface to replenish his breath.

At the instant he bobbed back onto the surface, he heard one of the bangs, this time much closer, and instantly felt a rush of air to the left of his neck and was pushed sharply and painfully to his right.

He now saw that one of the boats was in front of him, no more than thirty or forty puffin-lengths away. In the next few seconds, Aldar took in several things at once. Firstly, the bangs came from long stick-like objects the humans carried; secondly, one of the humans was scooping what were clearly dead birds out of the sea; and thirdly… the sticks were now pointing at him.

He didn't need any more warning and immediately dove beneath the sea, instantly "flying" under the water to his right and away from the nearest boat. He stayed under as long as he could, then rose only to take a quick breath before diving again, this time weaving sharply to his left but still away from the boat, which was now somewhat further behind him. Rising to the surface again, he immediately began to race along the water and took flight as soon as he had gathered sufficient speed. Flapping his small but powerful wings as fast as he possibly could, he put as much distance as possible between himself and the deadly humans. Even so, he heard several more bangs and, at one point, heard the high-pitched whistle of something passing his head no more than a bird's width away at a speed Aldar didn't know was possible.

Once again, our puffin had learned that humans equalled deadly danger. He also reappraised the suitability of this region for spending the winter and headed west and slightly north into the open ocean. The very worst that winter and its tempestuous weather could throw at him was nothing compared with the terrible danger that emanated from humans at every turn.

16

Arctic

The sky was awash with meandering curtains of coloured light

Both the air and the sea were getting colder as Aldar continued north and west, but the decreasing length of days was even more noticeable. The fishing was still good, and although the frequency and intensity of storms were increasing slowly, the puffin was now more than able to ride these out as long as the fish were not driven too deep nor scattered too widely.

Many days later, Aldar sighted land once more to the west. This appeared to be much larger than the small islands he had last visited, and much higher. Aldar could already see high mountains often shrouded in cloud and capped with glistening white glaciers. He wasn't interested in such inland features, though - there would be no fish there. His only interest in the land at the moment was to know if men were present, if the currents around the main landmass or its surrounding reefs and smaller islands were places where there was abundant fish and other food, and if, once again, he could find sheltered waters in the lee of any such islands. For a few short days, Aldar was content to sit on the surface of the cold, grey sea, gradually drifting closer to the landmass. There were plenty of fish but, for reasons he was unable to fathom, he needed to spend more time hunting even though he was making good catches. He had noticed that the type of fish had changed and wondered if somehow these were "the wrong type of fish." Aldar, of course, didn't think in terms of nutrition and calorific value - just whether the fish were good or bad. He remembered that the fish he had caught in the south were fat, oily, salty, and delicious, and kept a newly fledged puffin growing and strong.

Here, the fish were undoubtedly plentiful, but a puffin needed to hunt much more often to satisfy his hunger, and he wondered if this was something to do with this particular area. He could sense currents from the south that felt somehow "wrong", maybe this was also affecting the fish. Once again, raw instinct took over, and Aldar turned north once more, hoping to encounter, "better" fish.

Keeping the wall of land always to his left, the puffin travelled on and off in a general northerly direction for many days. Many times, he came upon others of his species, and sometimes they would settle into a raft for some days, fishing together silently but nevertheless feeling a comradeship and togetherness that comes from shared genetics and shared experience. This was similar to, but more pronounced and comprehensive than, the sense of a shared place in the world he had experienced with the giant sea creature in whose eye he had seen a recognition of a fellow fish hunter. It may have been that the surprise of sharing such a feeling with such a physically different creature rendered it more intense. Always, though, after a few days, the raft would drift apart, and the puffins would return to their solitary lives at sea.

The days had now shortened to almost nothing, this part of the world in winter becoming a place of constant night. The long nights, though, were far from just dark, instead creating a stage for dramatic light shows when the sky was awash with meandering, glistening curtains of coloured light. These would appear soon after the sun returned into the sea from its brief climb into the sky. It never climbed very high and never stayed very long in the sky, sometimes barely rising above the high, glacier-topped mountains. The lights would ebb and flow for many hours, sometimes totally obscuring the stars with their shimmering display. Aldar soon grew used to them and the eerie illumination they created beneath the waves when he fished. Whether they shone or not, though, Aldar, with his excellent night vision, was able to fish, and the fishing was good - the prey juicy, fat, and succulent.

As he went further north, the balance of the fish changed again, away from the "bad" fish to more and more of the fat, delicious, and filling "good" fish. Along with this change, the numbers of both fellow puffins as well as other seabirds increased.

Then one day, while sitting in a raft of others, Aldar felt a frisson of fear run through the whole group. This emanated most strongly from those birds who were native to these seas and had fledged from the land just to the west. Looking towards the shore, he saw once again the small boats containing the humans and their long sticks from which the deadly explosions came. Already he had heard several of the sharp pops he knew meant that death could come to those at whom the sticks were pointing. He did not need those boats to get any closer to know it was time to leave again. Ever since he had seen the land, he had been wary of such floating carriers of danger, and it took only this one sighting to prompt him to leave the vicinity as fast as his short wings would carry him.

The wind was blowing strongly out of the west, the direction from which the men had come, so, unable to turn west again, Aldar turned directly east and, with the wind behind him, made his escape. This time, our puffin did not fly and swim further north but kept the same latitude, moving only east. He now felt he had seen the extreme west of the oceanic world, and seemingly going north would lead only to an ever colder, darker world. So he let the prevailing wind and current provide most of the forward impetus, carrying him back east and closer to his home colony.

The seas here were largely free of humans and their ships and boats and, although cold and stormy, were again rich in fine fishing. As the year passed through midwinter and the days began, at first only immeasurably slowly, to lengthen, Aldar turned his back on the west and the dangers posed by men. He had come to feel that the open ocean was the best place for a puffin - more exposed to the tumultuous winter tempests, perhaps, but at least free from the dangers posed by humans and their contraptions. Only as the days grew increasingly warm and long and the nights shorter did Aldar finally see land ahead of him once again. He was not to know that in these regions men were no longer allowed to hunt puffins, so he turned away from the land, and once far out to sea again, he halted his eastward drift and settled into life in the vast expanse of the Norwegian Sea.

Aldar had passed his second winter and survived, once again, the many hazards faced by a young puffin. He had, almost literally, come full circle - from the storms of the North Sea, through a journey south, then north and west, encountering danger from men several times, and finally turning east. There was only the final journey back south into the North Sea to complete his passage through his juvenile explorations, but he was still not ready for this.

17

Return to Flamborough

A place of high limestone cliffs topped with rich deep soil and lush green vegetation

Summer and winter have passed again for Aldar. He has not moved out of the Norwegian Sea in that time, content to remain where the fishing was good and the skies high and wide. There have been storms in that time, some as severe as the first Aldar encountered. There have also been fleeting encounters with men and their boats, but he has stayed as far away from them as he could. On a few occasions, he has also seen the signs of the deadly, shimmering nets which hang beneath the surface of the sea, but again, he has gained enough experience to steer clear.

His bill has also grown considerably over the past years and developed some of the characteristic grooves and colours of a full adult. He enters this, his third summer, with not quite the full breeding colouration of his beak and plumage, but not too far away. With these changes has also come an urge to be with his own kind again for a time. He is not ready for breeding, but he is ready to return to his birthplace on the northeast coast of England.

Aldar was born at Flamborough, a place of high limestone cliffs topped with rich, deep soil and lush green vegetation. The cliffs themselves are riven with cracks and crevices, perfect for a puffin to find a safe nesting place, or deep snug burrows can be excavated in the soil above. Our puffin was raised in a burrow deep in the brown soil just above the limestone cliff, and he will, by preference, seek out the same when it is time for him to breed. For this year, though, he will be content to loiter on the edges of the colony and in the rafts at sea, observing and learning more about life as an adult, breeding puffin.

In early March, driven by instinct as the days lengthen and the temperatures rise, he began his journey home. How he knew the way he was not sure - a complex mix of a mental map of the sea, the way in which the smells of the North Sea vary by region creating a scent map in which he knew the location of his birth colony, and some elements of navigating by the sun and stars. We humans would call the whole mix "instinct" and indeed it was not something Aldar had to think about or learn - he simply knew the way home.

After journeying for many days, he finally sighted, on a windswept, rain-washed day at the end of March, the cliffs he left behind three full years ago. It was one of those days when the freezing wind was blowing from the north, bringing late flurries of snow and cold, hard sleet. The sea was spumescent from the breaking waves, and the noise, as they continually spent their fury at the foot of the cliffs, was like a constant and unrelenting peal of thunder. Many startlingly blue-eyed gannets, brown guillemots, sharp-suited razorbills, and the dashing white kittiwakes had already arrived, as had numerous adult puffins.

Aldar simply knew the way "home".

Aldar joined a raft of puffins on the sea in front of the high and rugged cliffs, and for some time they rose and fell with the waves in silent harmony, occasionally being covered with wet snow but still warm under their thick and well-oiled plumage.

Over the next few days, and eventually weeks, Aldar observed the adult birds from a variety of vantage points, both on the sea and around the colony on land. On the sea, the rafts of puffins were completely silent, but once on the cliffs, the birds added to the cacophony from the other seabirds with their growls and grunts. He soon recalled that a puffin colony is a noisy, busy place and that, if he were to avoid a fight - particularly with adults in front of their own burrows - he needed to pass by with head held low and eyes averted. In this way, he communicated, "I'm just passing by, please excuse me."

Some of the puffins had already reunited with their partner from previous years, and these rejoined pairs would sit together and mate on the ocean before heading off to the burrow they had occupied twelve months ago. Others were still waiting or had yet to pair, and these waited longer in the raft. After waiting for some time, any male puffin waiting for his mate would leave the raft and fly to the pair's burrow, where he would call with a deep grunting sound to ensure his mate could find him, stopping only once she arrived safely. Some, a small number in a normal year, would wait in vain, their respective partners having failed to survive the winter for one reason or another.

Once on land, the pairs would sit together and reaffirm their lifelong bond with tender rubbing and clicking together of their beautifully adorned, multicoloured beaks. Aldar was careful not to get too close to these courting pairs and was also careful to give their nest site a wider berth once they had mated and the female had laid the egg deep in the earthy depths of the burrow. An inquisitive young puffin straying too close to a burrow with an egg, or later a young chick, was likely to receive a severe display of gaping, if not a beating, from the offended parents, and being tumbled helter-skelter down the sheer cliff face was something Aldar was keen to avoid.

And so, Aldar spent the summer largely in the company of other unattached puffins, observing the breeding adults and absorbing much that would be of use to him when it was his turn to be a parent. For him, the summer was one of lazy lingering on the densely populated cliffs or in rafts on the green and plentiful sea. Food was plentiful, and Aldar had only himself to feed, not a hungry, growing puffling. As far as he could tell, the parents this year managed to find enough fish within a short flight to feed themselves and their chick, even as it became hungrier with the passing weeks. The visits needed to increase to twelve times per day or more, and Aldar was aware that this rendered both parents extremely busy. Working together, though, they appeared to manage very well, and the season was a good one for chick survival. Aldar's experience of the vagaries of fish availability, though, gave rise to a suspicion that this might not always be the case.

The long summer days with no parental responsibility enabled the young puffin to observe the myriad other dangers the breeding adults faced in rearing their young. Herring gulls would chase the returning birds and force them to drop their precious catches of fish. Outlying, vulnerable burrows were sometimes raided by stoats, foxes, or rats, with the egg or the young chick being dragged out of the safety of the interior to provide food in turn for the young of these creatures. The summer breeding season was a time of new births for all species, many of which were hunters in their own right. Puffins may be hunters of fish, but they are certainly not apex predators and so had many who saw them - and particularly their pufflings - as food for their own young. An important lesson for a young prospective parent was to select a nesting site in a place as unreachable from land as possible and as near the centre of the colony as could be had. Competition for these, Aldar saw, was fierce, and the best sites went to early arrivals and/or dominant males.

Nor were dangers from the air confined to fish thefts.

One fine sunny day in the middle of the season, Aldar was sitting idly on the cliffs, occasionally nodding his head to other puffins or walking to and fro with the comical gait only a puffin can achieve. As he gazed out to sea, watching other birds fly off to fish or return with beaks stuffed with rows of beautiful, glossy sand eels, he became aware of an increase in the usual background tumult of calls, grunts, and cries. Many birds took to the air in just a few short seconds, plunging headlong for the relative safety of the sea, as a huge white-bellied bird flew over the colony. One unfortunate puffin, however, was too late in taking to the air, and the great bird dropped like a falling rock, straight onto it as it took off. Snatching the doomed puffin from the air, the predator flew off with it still struggling but held firmly in the webbed but sharply clawed feet of its captor. As it flew away with its unfortunate victim, Aldar saw that it was similarly coloured to a herring gull, but much darker (pure black) on its back and much larger. Humans would call this bird a great black-backed gull, and indeed it registered in the puffin's mind as the Great Black-Backed Killer - just one more threat to add to the ever-increasing tally of dangers faced by a small seabird.

74

Once midsummer was past and the days began to shorten once more, the weather turned increasingly unsettled and blustery, and rainswept days began to replace the calm sunny days of early summer. More and more pufflings were making their first hazardous flight as Aldar had done some three seasons ago, and the population of both puffins and other seabirds in and around the colony was decreasing daily as more and more took to the sea and did not return to the cliffs. The gannets still flew past in their aerial waves to and from their own colony on the steeper, higher cliffs a little to the north, and many of the kittiwakes were still busy feeding their young. Most of the puffins, though, and large numbers of the lusciously brown-feathered guillemots and the blacker-clothed razorbills had already left.

Aldar now had a decision to make about the coming winter: whether to stay in the stormy but relatively close North Sea, to journey south to the warmer but still tempestuous Bay of Biscay, or indeed to fly back north to the colder climes of the Norwegian Sea. He sensed his years of youthful wide-ranging wanderings were coming to an end, and so decided to stay in the seas not too far from the colony. Maybe next year he would be ready to find a female partner and together raise the first of, hopefully, many pufflings of their own.

18

Breeding Behaviour
1 Courtship

Clicking of beaks is an essential part of pair bonding.

Adult puffins will return to the colony where they hatched in their third or fourth year but do not usually find a partner until their fourth or fifth year. Courtship and, indeed, breeding usually take place on the sea before a pair will come on land to return to their burrow or to build a new one.

Puffins, in common with other seabirds such as guillemots and razorbills, will form rafts of large numbers of birds in the sea just offshore from the colony, at first only tentatively coming ashore for short periods before returning to the safety of the sea. How puffins select a partner is not known, although it is likely to be associated with the strength of the breeding colouration as well as size and dominance. The breeding colours are costly to maintain and indicate a puffin in good health and a proficient hunter, both traits being positively correlated with successful parenting.

Once a mate is selected, the pair will bond using elaborate rituals of beak rubbing and clicking. This bonding will be repeated frequently throughout the pair's life together. This is important as the birds spend many months of the year apart, only coming together in mid-March for a new breeding season. Immediately prior to mating, the male puffin will display by rapidly vibrating his outstretched wings, signalling to the female to allow him to mount her to mate.

Once partnered, puffins mostly breed for life, divorce rates are typically only around ten percent in any season. Infidelity rates are even lower and have been measured in one study as actually at zero.

19

Finding Agata

Aldar had grown into a strong flyer.

As autumn stretched into winter, Aldar remained on the North Sea, weathering the infrequent storms in what turned out to be an abnormally mild season. The availability of fish throughout the winter months remained at reasonable levels - not exceptional, but adequate for a puffin's needs - so that Aldar was in good condition as winter drew to a close and spring approached. At this point, he knew he would have a short period of time when he moulted and replaced his wing feathers, and he needed to have sufficient nutritional reserves for this to be successful. During this time, he would be completely flightless and would also be less effective at hunting and more vulnerable to predators from below. The moulting period was a difficult one for a puffin, as it is for all birds; the growth of efficient, undamaged, and fresh flight feathers, though, was an essential annual rejuvenation. This refreshing of his feathers had occurred at the end of Aldar's last two winters, but this time he noticed some wide-ranging and significant changes as the vulnerable period of moulting ended.

As his strong new wing primaries grew, the young adult puffin noticed that his colouring was, for the first time, becoming that of a full breeding adult. His facial feathering was completely white apart from a small amount of fading to grey at neck level, and he developed the distinctive, startlingly bright yellow, red, and orange additions to his beak. He also added horny patches around his eyes and the fleshy yellow rosettes at the corners of his mouth, while his legs and feet changed to a bright orange. He approached the coming breeding season with the supreme confidence born of relative youth and pride in his new adult form.

Now in full breeding attire, Aldar made his way back once more to the cliffs from where he had launched himself precariously into his juvenile life. This season was, however, completely different from the last; no more mere loitering for Aldar. He was eager to find a mate and so, as soon as there was a hint of the temperatures rising, he set off to complete the relatively short journey home to eagerly join the rafts of puffins looking for a mate.

In the course of his juvenile travels, he had grown into a strong flyer, but flying was still hard work. His wings were not like those of the gannets and gulls he had seen gliding effortlessly on the air currents; Aldar needed to flap hard and fast to remain airborne, so it was often easier, unless he had to move quickly, to just sit on the surface of the water and paddle with his strong legs and webbed feet. On his long journeys, he had always combined paddling with shorter periods of flight. But now his desire to find a female was strong, so he paddled fast, got himself above the water, and ran along the surface before using his strong wings to get airborne. Gaining speed rapidly, he flew fast and low over the waves, enjoying the exhilarating sense of freedom, his mature strength and health, and the anticipation of finding a mate.

The journey continued for only a few days. Aldar rested at night and fed frequently by dropping clumsily onto the sea to hunt for sand eels, sprats, or other small and delicious fish. He had never mastered the art of the graceful landing, and each time he either crashed into the crest of a wave or simply stopped flying and belly-flopped onto the water. Once he landed, though, he was just as at home on and under the sea as he was in the air, and would dive and feed until satisfied. He would then rest a few hours before taking to the air and continuing his progress towards the colony.

Eventually, there came a day when he knew he was nearing, once more, the cliffs of his home colony, with the dense rafts of many puffins on the water before them. At first, Aldar simply joined a raft, reacquainting himself with the company of others of his kind as he had the previous year. He could see many other adults, some paired, some waiting for a partner, and some, like himself, looking to find a new partner. The majority of this latter group were newly fully adult like Aldar, each sporting their bright new uniform with a certain swagger, but a few were adults whose previous partners had not returned. Aldar knew that once he found his mate, he would enter a relationship that would be for life; separation was rare amongst puffins, although not entirely unknown. There were extremely rare instances where, if one member of a pair proved to be inadequate in the essential skills of fetching food for the growing puffling, the other partner would abandon the pairing to seek an alternative. After only a short time adjusting to a social environment, as distinct from the deep solitude of the winter months,

Aldar felt ready to make his move. He had assessed his competition and was naively confident in his ability to attract a healthy, strong young mate.

Taking to the air, Aldar circled the raft of birds several times, looking for a likely female. He could see that there were groups of reunited pairs happily billing (rubbing and clicking their bills together) and several other mature males in the group making the deep grunting noise to attract their partner when she arrived. On the outskirts of the raft, there was a group, similar to himself, of newly matured puffins with several unattached females amongst them.

He headed that way, mentally preparing himself for a graceful, impressive landing - and promptly crashed into an unexpected wave, tumbling forward and under the water. He bobbed back to the surface, shook his head, and tried to re-establish the air of calm dignity he had been striving for. Puffing himself up to look as impressive as he could, he paddled over to one female who seemed to be alone, waving his head from side to side, an action he knew would invite billing. She seemed to be an older bird, probably recently widowed, and Aldar thought he might have a better chance of successful rearing with an already experienced partner. Sadly, she took one look at him, recognised his relative immaturity, and turned her back, rejecting his advances.

His supreme and arrogant bubble slightly deflated, he tried several other approaches, but each one was rebuffed. Aldar was beginning to feel dejected, having to dig a little deeper each time to find the bravado to puff himself up and make an approach. But just as he was about to take a break to soothe his damaged ego, he noticed one female sitting slightly apart from the group. She looked to be young, no older than he was, but she seemed strong and had beautiful breeding colours on her beak, eyes, and face. A large part of puffin recognition is by smell, and this female had a distinctive, healthy scent - a combination of sea and fish and fresh, well-groomed plumage. Another young male saw where Aldar was looking and gave him a look that seemed to say, "Don't bother with her, mate. Several of us have tried, but she rebuffs everyone - snooty bird she is."

Aldar, though, was intrigued by this young female with such attitude and decided to try a slightly modified approach: less dominance signalling and a bit more humility as a first-time breeder. He swam slowly towards her, looking this way and that as if not noticing her, and only when just a few feet away did he look straight at her as if to say, "Oh, I've only just seen you there." He moved his head to one side, waiting to see if she would respond, but nothing happened for several moments. He was about to give up, but he was very interested in this slightly strange female, so he tried another shake of his head. Still no response - and then, just as he was about to turn away, he noticed a tentative movement of her own head.

Finding Agata.

He waved his head again, more strongly this time, and she responded with a definite shake of her own head. Aldar swam a little closer, still tentatively waving his head from side to side, and to his delight she responded in kind. They were now moving their heads with an almost hypnotic synchronised swaying motion, and after several minutes of this, Aldar, plucking up all his courage, swam closer and pushed his beak towards hers. With his bruised self-esteem expecting her to change her mind and turn her back, Aldar held out his beak, inviting her to do the same. The first touch of her bill on his was tentative but electrifying, and he slid his beak over hers, feeling the pronounced grooves alongside the brightly coloured stripes. He then moved his head to do the same on the other side, and to his delight she responded in like fashion. They continued this tentative courtship for some time, with both caressing beak on beak and clicking their beaks together repeatedly. Aldar was delighted; he had found a slightly strange but strong, obviously well-bred and colourful young female, and she was clearly reciprocating the desire to bond.

Several other males, seeing that someone had apparently impressed this aloof female, began to approach the pair. They made as if to stand on the water, puffing themselves up with a display of dominance intended to scare Aldar away, but the female turned away from them and towards Aldar, making it clear that she had made her choice. The newly bonded pair swam, in unison, away from the group to continue the courting rituals in peace. In Agata, Aldar was sure he had found his mate for life and that this was just the beginning of a relationship which would last many, many years.

20

Breeding Behaviour 2 Nest Building

Not all nest material is appropriate.

The Atlantic puffin nest is made either at the inner end of a metre-long burrow in soft soil, or in a crevice in the cliff face. The new hatchling has a strong aversion to light and so will stay well hidden at the depths of this burrow or crevice. A shallow burrow or cleft is more likely to result in predation of the hatchling, so there is intense competition for suitable sites.

Most puffins nest on small offshore islands where there is less risk of land-based predators, at least until rats, cats, or similar are introduced by humans. There are a few mainland colonies in the UK, such as at Flamborough Cliffs in North Yorkshire. The puffin's nest is usually either deep in a cleft in rugged cliffs or in a burrow in soil on top of such cliffs. The burrow will sometimes be a rabbit burrow - either an abandoned one or one from which the unfortunate rabbit has been evicted. (Rabbits are no match for an aggressive puffin with its hard, sharp beak.) In the absence of such a burrow, the puffin pair will dig their own. In the latter case, the male will often do most of the digging while the female sits at the entrance, often being showered in soil excavated by the male. Digging takes place in bursts of a couple of hours, followed by feeding and mating, and will take several weeks to complete. The final tasks in creating a burrow are the widening of the nest chamber itself and the creation of a small side chamber in which the chick will defecate, helping to keep the main chamber and tunnel relatively clean. The nest itself is formed of dried grass, moss, sticks, and feathers.

The position of the burrow is an important indicator of breeding success, with those burrows nearer the centre of the colony being favoured. These sites are highly competed for and usually taken by early arrivals, leaving latecomers to nest on the outskirts where they are more vulnerable to predation.

21

House Hunting

The celebrated by sitting on the limestone ledge.

After several days of intense courtship and, ultimately, mating at sea, our new pair flew to the cliffs to select a site and prepare a nest. Aldar had been hatched in a burrow in the soft soil at the top of the rugged limestone cliffs, but Agata had, by contrast, begun life in a deep crack in the cliff face itself.

The pair searched the cliffs for a suitable and unoccupied crevice, beginning as near the centre of the colony as possible. As a new coupling, they were relatively late coming ashore, though, and so found all the suitable holes near the centre already occupied by indignant puffins. Several times, approaching what they thought was an empty fissure, they met with a robust stamping of feet and the gaping beak of one or both actual occupants. As they moved further and further away from the centre, they encountered fewer rival birds but also felt more in danger from predators. They changed tack and looked for either a suitable existing hole or a site where one could be dug, in the deep brown clay which sat atop the limestone. They avoided the damp, water-oozing sections, which would be unstable and likely to collapse into the sea, carrying any unwary nesting birds or chicks with them, and looked for sites with a good covering of grass or where there was dry, bare earth behind a small landing of limestone. After some exhausting days of searching, they found just such a site, which appeared not to be taken, and set about making it their own. First, though, they celebrated their success by sitting on the limestone ledge and clicking beaks adoringly and triumphantly for a short period. Just as with humans, the first flush of a newly formed partnership required physical contact, and continually renewing their new bond was an important part of developing a partnership that would be successful and long-lasting.

With great enthusiasm, they commenced the task of digging the new burrow, Aldar taking the lead and chopping away at the earth with his sturdy new beak. Before long, it was no longer the pristine, brightly coloured beak of breeding colouration he had come to the colony with but was stained and muddy from his efforts. Once he had loosened earth, he would clear it away by sweeping it behind him with his also muddy feet. Several times, he caught Agata full in the face with a load of shovelled soil as she sat at the entrance to the growing tunnel, but she would merely shake herself and look at him fondly and encouragingly. He didn't do all the digging, though, as she took turns at the arduous task, and at the end of each long day of digging, the two birds would fly out to sea to clean themselves and fish. Working as a pair, they completed the burrow to their satisfaction in just seven days or so and began both to widen the innermost end into a small cavern and then to line it with grasses, feathers, or other stuff they felt would make a snug and dry base for their egg and eventually for the single chick they would hatch.

With great enthusiasm he commenced the task of digging.

As they had been digging, they had also mated many times, Aldar climbing onto Agata's back in a comical but efficient process. Both were delighted with this and would click bills repeatedly afterwards, again always strengthening the all-important pair bond. They would need that strength of relationship all too soon.

Eventually, after some weeks, Agata retired into the burrow and emerged having laid a beautiful creamy white, slightly freckled egg. Aldar couldn't believe the size of it… nearly a fifth of the size of his mate. She immediately set off to feed, leaving the first egg-sitting session to him. That was OK, though, he was immensely proud of her and knew she'd be back soon enough to take her turn whilst he went off to hunt. As he sat patiently on the egg, he contemplated how he had come so far. From surviving his first storm, through many adventures at sea, and now to this place and time, about to rear his own firstborn. He thought of all the times he had survived what could have been catastrophic situations and all the things he had seen. He remembered again that his greatest threat came not from the weather or from gulls, foxes, weasels, and the like, but from the humans who seemed to destroy everything they encountered with so little apparent care. He wondered how soon the chick now developing in the egg beneath him would encounter these supremely dangerous animals; he could only hope the inevitable encounters were not fatal ones.

Several hours later, Agata returned to relieve a now-hungry Aldar, and he was able to set out to sea to feed himself. Without hesitation, he went to the fishing grounds they had been using since they arrived back at the colony some weeks ago, settled on the water - in his usual inelegant fashion, of course - and set about the hunt. The sea was quite calm, with only a slow rolling swell; the water, like a dark mirror, reflected the moon and stars above, reminding Aldar of the night in the Arctic when he had encountered the whale. Keen to enter hunting mode and then to feed, he first put his head under to check for predators and then, with a kick of his feet, he dived under the surface and was soon powering his way in search of the sand eels which had been numerous in this area.

Aldar was a skilled hunter, and once he sighted a shoal, he would be able to catch his fill with a few dives. This time, though, the fish were somewhat more thinly spread, meaning he had to work a little harder to satisfy his hunger, but this was not the first time the population of prey fish had changed, and he was sure he would find other, richer fishing grounds without too much trouble.

On landing on the narrow limestone ledge in front of the burrow, he first walked this way and that, stamping his bright orange feet and bobbing his head in the breeze. His gait was comical to observe but nevertheless conveyed the message that this was his territory and that his home and himself, as a soon-to-be father, should be treated with due respect. "This is my burrow," he was saying proudly to those who were looking.

Aldar's performance was disturbed by one slightly confused puffin who came darting in from the sea and tried to land on the small limestone platform which Aldar regarded as his front doorstep. In the instant he landed, though, he was dislodged and thrown back off the cliff by the sturdy homeowner. The intruder tumbled comically backwards before twisting acrobatically in mid-air and flying back out away from the cliff to make another, hopefully more accurate, attempt to land. As Aldar would learn, such encounters were not unknown as a puffin coming in from a long flight simply mistook one ledge for another, perhaps in haste to avoid a rampaging herring gull. He made some perfunctory growling calls to announce his "victory", and with a nod of satisfaction, he made his way down the metre-long tunnel to greet Agata. Clearly now hungry again herself, she spared him only a few moments of beak tapping before she was off, leaving him to brood the precious egg. Aldar wondered whether she too had found the fishing to be a little more challenging so that she had returned to the nest not quite satiated. He resumed his place on the egg, giving it a quick turn, and settled back to spend time with his own thoughts, deciding at length that next time he went to feed he would spend a little more time looking for new shoals rather than simply returning to the familiar grounds. With that, he tucked his beak under his wing, closed his eyes, and dozed, only occasionally twitching as his mind continued to revisit past hunting dives and rehearse and revise his skills. He and his partner had quickly settled into the next phase of this, their first, year's breeding activity. The next phase would be tougher on them both.

22

Rearing, Egg and Hatchling

A puffin's egg weighs some fifteen percent of the body weight of the female.

Puffins lay a single egg each year, which is incubated by both parents for around forty days before it hatches. The egg is a significant size compared with the body of the female, around ten to fifteen percent of her body weight, at around sixty one millimetres long and forty two millimetres wide, and weighing around sixty two grams That's the equivalent of a typical human female giving birth to an eleven kilogram baby! The egg is creamy white with a variable amount of light brown streaks and blotches.

The newly hatched chick takes approximately a week to gain its full covering of fluffy down, and during this time the parents must continually keep it warm; both have featherless brood patches on their lower belly to aid with this. During this time, the non-sitting parent will begin the task of bringing food for the chick.

Once the chick can maintain its own body temperature, both parents will hunt for fish, and the chick will be left alone in the nest for long periods of time. The availability of suitable food is a key factor in rearing success and can vary from one season to the next.

Both fishing activity by humans and human-induced climate change have a dramatic impact on breeding success. In the last twenty years, several colonies in the south of Iceland have seen almost zero breeding success as the commonly available sand eels were replaced in the warming waters by much less nutritious butterfish. In addition, those warmer waters can bring with them large populations of predatory fish, such as mackerel, which compete with the puffins for available fish stocks.

Finally, of course, human overfishing is also a major issue, with sand eels still being fished on an industrial scale, mainly by Denmark but also to a smaller extent by Norway and Germany, to provide animal feed and even fertiliser. The main fisheries are within UK waters, and in 2024 there were moves to ban such fishing to protect the declining seabird populations, including puffins. This is just one example of human-induced degradation of the environment, which continues to cause harm to many species; seabirds are just one group who struggle to survive in the face of the voracious appetite of Homo sapiens.

23

Puffling

The chick was small but already had a huge appetite.

The sky was a brilliant azure, with the sun shining warmly even though it was mid-evening. The days were lengthening towards their maximum, and the weather had been settled but unseasonably hot for the past few weeks whilst Aldar and Agata brooded their first egg. The length of the day didn't matter that much to the parents-to-be; with their night vision, they could hunt for fish in the dark or the light. The stifling heat, though, had made sitting in the nest chamber challenging for a bird used to life on the cold northern seas.

Aldar emerged into the clean, sea-scented air and breathed deeply and satisfyingly before setting about his routine of marking out his territory in the crowded colony. Strutting this way and that on his doorstep with intermittent displays of stamping and nodding his head, accompanied by deep grunts and even the occasional clicking of beaks, he exchanged evening pleasantries with those of his neighbours who were also on the cliffs. He had been relieved by Agata just a short time ago after a long shift on the egg; it would appear she, as well as he, was having to fly quite some distance to find the fish that were not only the mainstay of their diet but would also provide the vital sustenance for the growing puffling. Aldar wasn't sure why, but the shoals nearer to shore had all but disappeared, replaced by much larger shoals of herring and mackerel, themselves predators of the same smaller fish as the puffins. An additional strain on local supplies was, of course, driven by the high concentration of seabirds of all species who gathered at this location to breed. Competition for fish was high, and so the flights to feed were getting longer each day. Aldar hoped the situation did not worsen, as soon the chick would hatch and the need for fish would increase dramatically.

He stretched his wings, shook his head, and stamped his feet one more time before walking to the edge and launching into the late spring air, which had been warmed by another long sunlit day. Before heading off to the fishing grounds, he flew first straight down to the glassy sea, perfectly still once again as there was barely a breeze. Landing amongst more of his kind as well as the guillemots and razorbills with whom the puffins shared the cliffs, he immediately felt the relief of cool water on his stiff little body and submerged for pure pleasure, weaving, twisting, and plunging straight down into the even cooler depths. There was not a breath of wind, so that with this unmoving and unstirred sea heated by the unrelenting sun, the water of the top few feet was warmer than Aldar had known, even compared with the Bay of Biscay much further south. Below those topmost few feet, though, there was almost a wall where the warm water was separated from much cooler depths. Relishing the cool, Aldar "flew" under the water for some moments before surfacing again. Out here on the sea there was none of the grunting or growling of the puffin colony on land, but it was nevertheless a place where a puffin felt the comradeship of other birds. Much as he relished the cool swim, though, he was hungry after his long day on the nest, so, without lingering too long, he paddled, then ran along the water, and finally thrust himself into the air and set off to find a meal.

Aldar's wings were stiff after so long sitting still, so he enjoyed the stretch and the release of tension in his muscles. He skimmed the tops of the wide, low rollers before climbing to his cruising altitude of just about ten metres and then flying in earnest to reach, as fast as possible, the place where he hoped to find fish to fill his belly. After an hour or so, he sighted a group of diving gannets who, he knew, would be feeding on mackerel and other species larger than he could manage, but not too long later he saw rafts of smaller seabirds floating on the sea, diving and obviously feeding. Unworried by the competition, he dropped unceremoniously onto the water between two other puffins and immediately took his first dive. The mental switch to hunting took place the instant he saw prey, and before long he had singled out his first meal and was moving in for the kill. As always, the first taste of fishy flesh set his tastebuds aflame and heightened his need for more. It had been quite a long flight, but here were fish aplenty for all.

Aldar remembered that before he left, he had seen the first hints of a crack in the egg and had felt the increased movement of the chick within as it began its journey into the world. He wondered if he might be a parent when he got back to the nest. He might even take a beakful of sand eels for Agata as a rehearsal for the days ahead of feeding the growing puffling. But first, he was sure he had room for several more tasty, oily, salty fish in his own belly. As the sun finally set with a glorious explosion of orange and gold in the west, Aldar dived beneath the waves once more.

Some time later, with his belly finally full, he dived one last time and filled his beak ridges with delicious sand eels before setting off back to the nest to relieve Agata. He noticed again that the flight was quite long and hoped that the shoals nearer shore might return before too long.

Near the end of his flight back to the nest, only a short distance from the shore, his vision was momentarily clouded by an ominous shadow and, looking up, he confirmed he was being stalked by a large herring gull. He knew that this much larger bird was highly likely to attack him in an attempt to get him to drop his catch so that it could take it for itself. This was a common occurrence for the puffins, and even though this time his mouthful was merely a gift for Agata, he was nevertheless determined to hold on to it. The puffins had several ways to try to protect themselves; the most commonly used was to gather on the sea and then make their way ashore in a large group, confusing the attacker. Aldar looked for a raft of gathering puffins below but could not see any just now, so he knew he was, this time, on his own and would have to try other avoiding strategies. He flew down close to the water, pretended to land but immediately ran along the surface and took to the air once again. The gull, though, was not going to give up so easily and was still above Aldar. It swooped down, feet extended, and tried to grab him, but Aldar tucked his head and in a split second dodged swiftly to the right, banked steeply, furiously flapping his strong wings, and then turned again sharply to the left. He turned again and again, ducking down and sweeping back up in an impressive display of aerial acrobatics. Finally, he headed straight for the cliff, only turning upwards at the very last moment. The gull, which was still in pursuit, had to apply full reverse thrust and at the same time turn away from the cliff to avoid a collision with the unyielding rock face. It squawked in frustration, but Aldar had, this time, been successful in evading the attack, and the gull returned to circling the colony, looking for a less agile puffin and one who was perhaps less willing to defend its catch.

Our puffin's last thought before putting the incident behind him and landing on his doorstep was just that with fish further out to sea and harder to find, the last thing they needed was also to be plagued by robber gulls.

Extending his feet before him as he approached the landing, he reduced speed by angling his wings into the oncoming airflow and attempted a graceful landing. As always, he failed and tumbled forwards onto his belly, though still holding tightly to his beakful of fish. With a quick, status-regaining shake of his head, he tucked his wings in and headed straight into the burrow, just in case the hungry gull was still within striking distance. He was immediately aware of a change, a change in the smell of the burrow and, he knew, a change in his life for the rest of this season at least. He and Agata would continue to need to brood the chick for a few days until its downy first coat of feathers dried and fluffed up fully to provide protection, but they would also now be fishing not just for themselves but for a newly hatched chick.

Approaching the nest chamber, he could make out Agata, but he couldn't yet see the chick - not until Agata climbed off the small gathering of sticks and feathers that constituted their nest. The chick was small and not yet fluffy, but with its huge eyes and gaping beak, once spotted it immediately got Aldar's attention. He dropped a few of the fish for the grateful Agata; that would be the last time he would be able to spare food for her until the chick fledged. He also took several more to the chick and, in response to its pecking, released them straight into its mouth. They were swallowed whole and without ceremony, and the feeding task of the two new parents had begun in earnest.

He bade farewell to Agata with a look that said, with as much eloquence as words would have, "Don't be long," and settled down with the newly hatched chick nestled under his body.

24

Rearing 2
Kleptoparasitism

A puffin can carry ten to twenty fish in its beak, an obvious target for predators.

Puffins bring food to the nest by gathering and holding the sand eels they have caught firmly in their beaks. They can hold many fish in place with the special adaptations of their beak and upper mouth, but they can be made to abandon their catch by the unwanted attention of larger birds such as gulls and skuas.

The attacking of puffins to rob them of their catch is known as kleptoparasitism. Common attacking species are herring gulls, skuas, and lesser black-backed gulls.

A Kelptoparasitic attack: -

A kleptoparasitic attack by a herring gull on a puffin is a dramatic and intense interaction often witnessed in seabird colonies, where both species coexist. In this scenario, let's imagine a successful escape by the puffin:

Setting:

This encounter takes place on the rocky cliffside overlooking the ocean, where a colony of puffins has long been established and where numerous puffins return from the sea with beaks brim full of sand eels to feed their chicks. Herring gulls, known for their kleptoparasitic behaviour, circle menacingly above, keenly watching for any opportunity to snatch a meal from the unwary, the careless, or simply the unfortunate.

The Approach:

Unlike outside the breeding season, when the puffins simply devour their catch safely in the open ocean, the puffins must feed their ravenous and growing chick and to do so must return to the colony with their mouths full of small fish. If a puffin, even momentarily, perches on a rock, perhaps preening its feathers or simply pauses too long before approaching its burrow, then the gulls will attack. Even in flight, the puffins are not safe, as a gull may launch a mid-air attack in the hope of forcing the puffin to lose its catch, to be swept up from the surface of the sea by the aggressor.

The Attack:

Seizing the opportunity, a herring gull will drop down from above, its sharp beak and webbed feet tipped with sharp claws extended towards its target. It will swoop on the puffin from behind, attempting to force it to drop the fish and escape - in other words, to steal the fish right from the puffin's mouth.

If this attack fails, the mugger might target a flying puffin and harass it in the air. In the face of such an attack, the much smaller bird will often be forced to let go of its catch to escape. Better to survive and be able to replace the lost food rather than risk injury or death.

Avoidance:

Puffins can evade attacks but will often fail to hang on to their catch. The main evasion tactic is for the birds to return to the colony in a mass, thus confusing the attackers and making it difficult for them to single out an individual bird. They will also rise en masse and circle above the colony, again providing confusion and distracting the gulls from selecting an individual target. These displays, known as "wheels", are a dramatic sight but one with a desperate purpose.

25

Struggle

Aldar was not going to lose his catch at the last moment.

Several days later, the food situation had not improved. Both Aldar and Agata had now lost several catches to the gulls, and to make things worse, the shoals of sand eels closer to the shore had not reappeared. The new parents were still managing the five feeds a day needed at that point, but only just, and Aldar was worried.

Another ten days later, returning from his latest hunting foray, he breathed a sigh of relief as he sighted the white cliffs ahead. It had been a long flight, far too long, and, once again, he had barely had time to catch enough to feed himself and to bring a full beakful back for the chick. Aldar also knew Agata was not managing to feed herself enough, and he could see she was growing thinner each time he saw her. He himself had, on several occasions, been forced to sacrifice his own feeding to return enough for the chick.

The distance to the fishing grounds and the difficulty finding the numbers of sand eels or sprats he needed, both to feed himself and to take enough back for the chick, was already a huge challenge, and he knew it was only going to become even more difficult as the chick, and its voracious appetite, continued to grow.

He approached the cliff and could see the entrance to their burrow, a dark hole in the pale brown soil which topped the white limestone. He dropped onto the small landing spot, as always only just hanging onto his load of fish as he stumbled forwards. He had not only dived up to two hundred feet under the waves to find and catch them, but he had also evaded two attacks by gulls on the way back, so he was not going to lose them now.

Taking a few short steps into the burrow, he paused and allowed himself a few moments for his eyes to adjust; already he could hear the excited, high-pitched calls of the chick as it sensed his arrival. The chick, no name yet, rushed to meet Aldar halfway down the tunnel, and the adult could feel him pecking at the fish in his beak. He quickly released each fish when it was pecked and could hear the chick gobble it down whole. After providing a few fish in this way, he dropped the rest of the catch onto the tunnel floor and set off back to the entrance, leaving the chick to hungrily snaffle the dropped fish.

Aldar could sense that the chick had been extremely hungry when he arrived, and although he knew it could last for many hours between feeds, he also knew that if it was to grow at the rate needed, he and Agata were going to need to make more successful trips each day than they were at the moment. If only the shoals nearer the shore would reappear or the predatory gulls cease their constant harassment, things would be easier.

The sun was still fairly low in the sky as he emerged into the golden early morning daylight, looking anxiously around to check for any threats. He took a few precious moments to preen, to stretch his tired wings, and to prepare for another flight before, stepping towards the cliff edge, he launched himself into the still cool air. He corrected for the growing wind and set off again for the fishing grounds, not knowing whether he would see Agata today. They had rarely seen each other since the chick had hatched, as they never knew when the other would return with fish. Aldar hoped they might both return to the nest at the same time at some point in the next day or so.

Although he was tired and hungry, barely having caught enough on the last trip, the journey out was uneventful. Arriving at the spot where he thought he was most likely to find the fish he desperately needed, he dropped down onto the sea and sat for a few moments, simply relishing the familiar pleasure of being back on the open ocean. But time was already pressing; this fishing spot was a long distance from the nest, and although he was a good flyer, his wings easily managing the number of beats per minute needed to keep him airborne, he knew the flight was too long to be able to make enough trips each day.

Diving down below the surface, his eyes quickly adjusted to the different density and lightscape of the water, and he set about finding his prey. Ducking, weaving, and darting this way and that, he used both his wings and webbed feet to pursue and catch any small fish that came within sight. He loved the chase, but right now he needed each attempt to be successful and short-lived, allowing him to rapidly fill the serrations on his beak with plump, nutritious morsels. He made dive after dive, each a little deeper, until finally he was diving to his full range of two hundred feet or so, in an effort to find the sand eels he knew should be there. Unfortunately, as on too many other occasions in the days since the chick had hatched, the prey simply was no longer present in sufficient numbers. He wondered if the huge ship he had seen had taken the whole shoal in its vast nets, leaving just the remaining few he was seeing. He feared those nets; to get caught in them was certain death, and he had seen them scoop up whole shoals of sprats and eels, along with dozens of hapless hunting puffins, before now.

It was time to move on. Wearily, he launched himself into the air and set about the search for more fish. Only after some considerable time did he spot the tell-tale signs of a new shoal and manage to feed himself and fill his beak for the journey back to the burrow; this was just not going to be good enough. He flew low and fast, sometimes even skimming the waves to try to stay hidden from the gulls, which he knew would readily rob him of his prize. Eventually, he made it back to the burrow and was in time to find Agata also present.

He fed the chick in the usual way and then greeted her. They clicked beaks and, with nodding heads, renewed the bond so newly formed this year. She looked tired, hungry, and not the plump, sleek female he had courted amongst the rafting birds a few short weeks ago. She too had only just returned and had not even managed a full beak of eels for the chick. It was clear that they were struggling to find enough food to feed their recently hatched chick.

Another week passed.

Hungry, tired, and in increasingly poor condition, Aldar returned to the nest again with a beak full of sprats for the chick. Agata was not there, and he knew he needed to set out immediately to fish again; unless something had miraculously changed, it would be many hours before he returned.

The chick had pecked, almost angrily, at his load of fish, clearly hungry, and he had released them into its gaping beak as fast as he could. He knew he and Agata were trying desperately to keep up the feeding regime, but he also knew their firstborn was just not growing as it should. Unless they could find more food quickly, they were in danger of starving themselves but, even as they did so, also failing to provide enough for the chick. Wearily, he set off once more as the last rays of the dying day lit up the sky and the thin scattering of clouds with a blaze of fiery red. Aldar, though, had no time, nor indeed the energy, to admire the sunset.

This time, he found a fishing ground in the same place as last time, but on returning to the colony he was unable, despite some desperate flying, to successfully evade the predatory attack of a herring gull. He was forced to make a second trip before he was able to return with a meal for the chick. When he did return, he was immensely pleased to find Agata also there, but seeing her for the first time in a few days, he was shocked at her appearance. She was getting terribly thin now and clearly weakening; her feathers were beginning to lose condition, and Aldar knew this could be fatal, as she needed the protection of that coat to stay dry, warm, and to fish successfully.

They clicked beaks, but without the ambitious optimism of their first days together. This desperate shortage of prey, together with the predations of the gulls, was taking a terrible toll on them both. Their bond was stronger than ever, but they were both fully aware that a dreadful decision was looming.

Without words, they agreed to go on for one more day; neither wanted to make the heartbreaking decision they already knew in their hearts was inevitable.

The following day, he managed four feeds but only by partially depriving himself of food. At one point, he had spotted a brilliantly large shoal of sprats. Quickly settling on the sea and diving beneath the surface, he was surprised not to be alone in hunting the fish but was instead surrounded by larger mackerel, many of them bigger than himself. There seemed to be an inexhaustible number of them, and they jostled and hustled relentlessly. Every time Aldar targeted a sprat, he had it snatched away at the last minute by the larger fish. Within minutes, the shoal had either been consumed by the mackerel or had scattered so that they presented an almost impossible challenge for the weary puffin. He managed to catch one or two, but nothing like sufficient to satisfy his own hunger, nor fill his beak for the chick. Once again, he had to resume the search for a fresh fishing spot. Finally, after far too many hours, he returned to the nest with only a few fish for the chick and settled down to wait for Agata. He knew now that the decision they dreaded had to be made. To stay alive themselves, they were going to have to leave for the deep Atlantic and leave the chick to starve.

Maybe next year they would be more successful.

Aldar's saddest day.

26

Fish

Puffling had given up hope of being fed again.

Fish...

The puffling stared at the opening to the burrow, wondering when either of his parents would return with food. He was very hungry by now. They had always returned in the past - not as fast as he would have liked, but always coming in the end. The thing puffling remembered most of all, the thing that seemed to have always been a haunting presence in his young life, was hunger.

It seemed like an eternity now since he had picked up the last of the fish his father had dropped on the rough earthen floor of the burrow and swallowed it whole. He could still taste the salty fleshiness of it, or at least he could remember it.

He was sure one or other of them would return soon.

Fish...

It was night now, and still no one had come with food. He thought he had been hungry before, but now he thought he knew what real hunger felt like. His young body was crying out for nourishment.

Where were they? What could have happened to delay them?

Puffling slept fitfully, never quite escaping the emptiness in his belly.

Fish...

Puffling woke and realised it was full day outside the burrow. He could hear the usual sounds of the colony - the grumblings of the adult puffins, the cry of the kittiwakes, the background roaring of the sea crashing against the base of the cliff so far below the burrow.

He was angry now. Where were they with his food? How dare they leave it so long? His belly ached with emptiness. He pecked at the walls of the burrow, wondering if that would assuage his hunger, but the bitter, earthy taste only made him retch.

He grabbed a beetle that scurried past and hungrily crunched and swallowed it. It did nothing to change the gnawing hunger.

Fish...

Night again now, and puffling had dozed through most of the day. His belly was now painfully bloated, and he could taste the acid in his throat as his body tried desperately to gain sustenance from anything it could.

Puffling was really frightened now. He could not understand what had happened to his world, his regular supply of life-sustaining food. He was also becoming dehydrated, as his sole source of water was the fish his parents brought him.

The burrow had been unbearably hot during the day; at least it was cooler now. Puffling pecked at any speck of anything that might be food. He was becoming desperate.

Fish...

Puffling woke in the night, hearing a sound at the entrance to the burrow. For a brief moment, he thought it might be one of his parents but soon realised it was just another bird sniffing the entrance and peering within to see if the burrow was empty. Maybe another puffin, or maybe a gull thinking there might be a meal inside. Puffling kept silent; he used to anticipate the appearance of his food-bearing parents with loud, high-pitched cheeps, but somehow, he knew this would only betray his unguarded presence to any predator.

He had given up hope now of being fed again and was fast growing weaker.

Puffling slept.

Fish…

It is day again, and there is no movement in the burrow.

Puffling never woke from that last sleep. His life cut desperately short as his parents realised, they simply could not bring enough food to enable their hatchling to grow. They had taken the only choice they could and had saved themselves for the chance to breed another year.

No Fish…

27

A New Season

Maybe this year would be more auspicious.

Aldar flew low over the raft of birds on the sea, not far from the cliffs of Flamborough where he and Agata had built their first nest and tried to raise their first chick. He would instantly recognise his mate and her scent, even though the last time he had seen her she had been thin, weak, and with feathers in poor condition. The struggle to feed their offspring in a year of near famine for puffins had reduced the strong, beautiful female puffin he had courted to an atrociously pale shadow of herself; they had parted with inconsolable sadness, having decided they must abandon the chick to save themselves.

Of course, as with every puffin, Agata would have faced the perils of a period where she was flightless whilst she moulted those old, tired feathers and renewed her vital plumage. She would have faced other dangers too: winter tempests, predators, the need to find food, and, of course, the dreadful perils brought by human activity. But Aldar was confident she would be back; she was a strong young bird and one, he knew, with great determination, reserves of courage, and strength of will.

He landed in the raft and set about locating his mate by her distinctive scent. Failing to find her after several hours, he set about assuaging the hunger that had built up as he covered the final miles to the colony without stopping to feed. The water here just offshore was shallow, and the rocky seabed was home to many crustaceans he had not tasted for some months, spending as he did the winter above the deeps of the Norwegian Sea. Diving beneath the choppy surface, he quickly found and gobbled several small pink crabs and delicious crispy shrimps. He was also relieved and delighted to see a healthy stock of sand eels even this close to their clifftop home; maybe this year would be more auspicious.

There was a strong breeze from the north, the weather was chilly, and the sea surface was flecked with white froth from waves whose peaks toppled in the wind even before they reached the shallows beneath the towering limestone wall at the edge of the land. Breaking through the spume after one more dive, Aldar was overjoyed to see - and smell - Agata waiting for him on the surface. She looked again like the bird he had first seen twelve months ago: plump, strong, sleekly feathered, and gorgeously healthy. With a mix of both relief and elation, the two puffins paddled close and immediately set about renewing their lifelong bond with a frenzy of bill clicking and head shaking.

This year they were sure they would not fail!

The next step was to reclaim the burrow they had made last year. There were no traces of the doomed hatchling when they entered for the first time - the scavengers had cleaned things up for them. They carried out some repairs where the tunnel walls had collapsed a little, cleaned out the old nest material, and added fresh twigs, feathers, and a little grass. A few days after renewing their partnership, Agata laid the precious, creamy white egg.

The season was a huge improvement on the previous one, with abundant fish relatively close to the colony. It may be that this was, at least partly, because of the cooler, wetter weather or the fact that the wind was more predominantly from the southwest than the south, bringing with it frequent rain. To our puffin couple, all that mattered was the prospect of being able to feed the growing chick.

After forty days, it was Aldar who witnessed the chick emerge, wet and bedraggled, from the egg and flop exhausted into the nest. Aldar removed the eggshell and other remains and immediately covered the hatchling with his warm body. It was essential to keep it warm in the first few days before its downy coating dried and fluffed into an insulating overcoat.

Before long, Agata returned and they both sat in joyful admiration of their new offspring for some time before Aldar set off to feed, leaving his mate to the brooding duties. Before taking flight, Aldar announced the hatching to the colony and reasserted his ownership of the burrow with a stamping dance on the doorstep. He waved his colourful beak in the air, growled, and stamped one glorious orange foot, then the other, repeating the process several times. He even clicked beaks with their immediate neighbour. Then, feeling every bit the proud father, Aldar threw himself from the cliff, swooping down towards the still choppy waters of the North Sea before powering into a swift horizontal flight. Seeing a raft of colony residents on the water just a short distance from the cliffs, Aldar could not resist landing amongst them and displaying again, with vigorous nodding of his head and waving of his spectacularly bright beak, his pride and prowess in hatching a new chick.

Finally, though, hunger and the knowledge of a hungry chick waiting back at the nest got the better of him, and he took to the air once more for the, thankfully shorter, trip to find sand eels. It wasn't long before he spotted the tell-tale signs and plonked down onto the cool water to begin hunting. His skills had continued to improve over the previous winter, so it wasn't long before, belly full of succulent morsels and with a beak stuffed with more, he set off back to the nest.

As he approached the rugged white shoreline, he was on the lookout for the predatory gulls but saw none this time. Maybe they had had their fill from other unfortunate birds, maybe they were just elsewhere along the coast - he didn't care. He returned to his doorstep no more than an hour after he left, his beak fully loaded with nutritious, tasty, life promoting fish.

Aldar ducked his head and headed down the tunnel to the nest chamber, where Agata was sitting patiently and contentedly on the nest, and offered her first choice of the meal he had brought back. She declined, however, still sated from her own hunting and preferring the first catch to go to the hatchling. The omens were good; she didn't want to do anything to disturb them.

Aldar left her on the nest and set out once more in the rapidly darkening evening to bring back another beakful.

Of course, nothing is perfect, and no season is without its challenges, and over the next few weeks there were times when the shoals retreated further from shore or were snatched away by human fishermen or larger fish. There were times when the gulls were ever-present, and there were times when the parents went hungry to ensure a good supply for the hatchling - but ensure a good supply they most definitely did. Overall, the hunting was good, and the hatchling grew fat and strong and began to replace the fluffy down with its first coat of juvenile feathers.

As the chick grew, so did its appetite, and Aldar and Agata were kept busier and busier as the days went by, each delivering nearly ten beakfuls of fish every day as well as feeding themselves. Tired, sometimes hungry, and always pressed for time, nevertheless they were proud, devoted parents.

After nearly forty days, they decided the hatchling was at peak weight and the time for it to fledge had come. They had been coaxing it to the entrance for a while by leaving some of their fishy deliveries near the top of the burrow. Aldar had coaxed it outside one calm, warm evening, but only after he had carefully surveyed the surroundings for predators and warned all the neighbouring puffins off with a solid display of stamping and even a beak-gaping threat towards one who allowed his curiosity to get the better of him, getting just that little bit too close. The youngster hadn't stayed out long, being nervous away from the close, comforting surroundings below ground, but it was a good start.

Some parents simply stopped delivering food at this time, leaving the young puffin with a stark choice: fledge or die. Aldar and Agata, however, had decided to remain with their treasured first fledgling until it was safely on the sea. And so, on the evening of that auspicious day, as the daylight faded to the golden tones of sunset and then the pale but darkening blue of night, they stood at the entrance and encouraged their fledgling out into the wide world. At the moment he emerged from the burrow, they gave him his name: Anor.

Aldar flew down to the calm blue-green sea, and Agata remained with Anor, gently coaxing him to make that perilous first leap. Anor stretched his wings, nodded his head at his mother, looked around at the world, and fearlessly propelled himself off the cliff. Like his father before him, neither his first flight nor his eventual collision with the waves was of any great elegance, but he survived and found himself floating naturally high in the water. Initially surprised at how cold it was and at how it moved constantly under him, he soon grew in confidence, and his father was there at his side to help him take the next and final step before they left him to make his own life, for better or worse.

That final step was to tuck his head down, dive beneath the surface, and begin the hunt for food. Watching Aldar closely, he followed him under the water and kept pace with him as he searched for prey. Fish of the right type weren't too abundant this close to the shore, especially after a season of fishing by thousands of puffins, but Aldar soon sighted one and switched into hunting mode. As ever, he melded his mind with the prey, following it this way and that, and finally pounced - not where the fish was, but where it would be in a fraction of a second. Then, with a snap of his powerful beak, the fish was his.

The lesson was repeated several times, but the time had come for Aldar and Agata to say farewell and good luck to their new, and now fully independent, son. With a final exchange of beak clicking, they both left Anor to make his own journey. Hopefully, a long and successful life lay in front of him, but the perils faced by a newly fledged puffin were many. Only Anor could overcome them; the bond with his parents was broken, and he was alone in the world.

Aldar and Agata spent some days either in a raft of other puffins or just by themselves, feeding and relaxing after their successful mission. This was hugely different to the closing of the previous breeding season, and both were elated at their success. This was a short time in which they renewed their lifelong bond and remade their commitment to meet again in the early spring of the following year.

At the end of a day when the weather had been particularly fair but beginning to be tinged with an autumnal feel, a glorious sunset lit the low but scattered clouds with an intense red and orange glow, as if the furnaces of the underworld had all been opened to the sky at once. Our puffin pair knew it was time to go their separate ways for the winter. They felt no concern, nor sadness; this was just as much a part of their life as the hectic teamwork of the breeding season, and they needed time alone to rebuild resources before the labours of raising another new chick.

With a last entwining of their beaks, they each departed - Aldar for the Norwegian Sea and Agata for who knows where. Aldar never knew and never asked where she spent her winters.

Anor.

28

Anton, Aran and Agneta

Aldar and Agata met again on a crystal-clear March morning.

In the following two years, Aldar and Agata successfully raised two more male pufflings, first Anton and then Aran. Each year had its own challenges and lessons, but each year brought a successful fledging. At the end of each year, our pair would spend a few days re-bonding after the hard work of the season before heading off on their own for the winter. Each year, as spring blossomed and the hours of daylight each day began to creep past those of darkness, they would meet again to renew their commitment to each other and begin again the process of cleaning the burrow and mating. They would bring in fresh nesting material, nurse Agata's precious single egg, and then begin the really hard work of feeding and nurturing the ravenous chick.

Their fifth season together brought some special challenges but also some particular joys. They met, on a glassy calm sea, on the morning of a cold but crystal-clear late March day. Both were still birds in their prime and both had spent an efficacious winter recuperating, feeding, and regaining the vital strength and resilience needed to see them through another breeding season. As always, each was delighted to see the other; Agata would always appear as Aldar was under the surface of the water fishing, so that it seemed to him that she could appear out of nothing - one second not there, and the next a familiar and still exciting presence beside him. He never knew which dive would be the one that ended with her almost magical materialisation, increasing his delight when he did return to the surface to find her there. This year was no different, and the two birds spent some time re-igniting their lifelong bond before setting about the task of getting the nest ready and, of course, mating frequently as they did so.

The large creamy white egg was duly laid by Agata, and the pair shared the sitting and the egg turning until the day of the hatching. The puffins were jubilant to find the emerging chick was their first female; Aldar was particularly thrilled at this, as bringing into the world another puffin like Agata was a long-nurtured ambition.

This season was far from an easy one, and it took longer than usual to bring the hatchling to the point of fledging. Firstly, there were several unseasonably severe storms soon after the hatching. Not only did the ferocity of the wind prevent either puffin from making the flight to the feeding grounds, but, as always after a severe storm, the prey fish were scattered or had migrated deeper into the ocean, beyond the diving ability of a puffin. The first storm was one of the worst Aldar had experienced, and the two had no choice but to sit it out in the mouth of their burrow and hope that it would soon dissipate so that they could resume feeding the chick before any lasting damage was done. The prey fish had only just begun to reappear in large shoals when a second convulsion swept in from the southwest. These were hard times, but the two battled through and managed to keep their precious daughter from starving, though the toll on themselves was hard.

Thankfully, there were no more severe storms after this, although the season did continue to be particularly wet and windy. Our birds, though, are more than capable of surviving a little rain and wind, as they are, of course, superbly adapted to the worst weather the northern seas can throw at them. Although the fledging would be late this season, Aldar and Agata both remained confident, and indeed extremely determined, that they would not fail to successfully release their beautiful female offspring into the world.

The second challenging feature of this breeding season to trouble the puffins was a particular preponderance of voracious predators. The colony was, as ever, plagued by the usual gulls but also, this season, by the appearance of a pair of buzzards that would sometimes take unwary adult birds and were certainly a threat to any chicks who ventured out of the burrow during daylight. The outer reaches and more accessible burrows were also robbed by a weasel, which made its appearance just as the chicks hatched and were at their most vulnerable. Aldar and Agata's burrow proved to be safe from this threat, as it was surrounded by slopes that were too steep and unstable to allow a land animal any access. With extreme good fortune, neither of the pair had a serious encounter with the buzzards but, of course, they faced the usual danger from herring gulls trying to steal their catch and from the occasional great black backed gull, which would, given the chance, take the adult bird itself.

Through all this, our pair brought their daughter to the day of fledging, and on a rare calm, clear but moonless evening, they encouraged the now mature, fat, and strong chick out into the world at large. Aldar checked even more carefully than usual for any threats, and Agata made her way onto the sea to welcome the fledgling as she entered the water. The sky above was a spectacular black dome arrayed with the piercingly bright cast of stars and planets as the young female was coached out from the entrance to the burrow. Since the season had seen so many predators, this was her first time fully outside, and Aldar could see the initial nervousness in her eyes. As she emerged fully, he gave her the name he and Agata had decided was most apt for their first daughter, and so Agneta was introduced to the future.

He encouraged her to the edge of the doorstep platform and, repeating the message, already often given - that the safest place for a puffin was on the sea - induced in her the courage to make the leap into the void and to try her wings for the first time.

After a short but tumultuous first flight, she landed on the sea just a short distance from Agata. Agneta had made the transition from chick to free-living puffin, ready to take on the world. After the traditional first few lessons in fishing, she would soon depart from the shore and, by morning, be far out in the North Sea, beginning her life and entering the first few years of adventures far from the colony. With luck and determination, she would return aged four or five to find a mate of her own and continue to bring strong, beautiful puffins to the ocean world.

And so, our two puffin parents relaxed once more and had time and space to spend the next few days feeding, diving, bobbing on the waves, and enjoying the lack of urgency to bring catch after catch to feed a hungry chick. They were, it must be admitted, very pleased with themselves and carried an indefinable glow of success with them.

The days were beginning to shorten and the nights to cool quickly, but the weather was finally calm, and so the pair were able to enjoy several days just relishing each other's company. On one unremarkable day among many, the two puffins, both well fed and at peace, spent the afternoon drifting gently with the current, now beginning to feel the growing urge to leave the locality of the colony and find again the solitude of the open ocean. The sun shone in a pale blue sky, flecked with only a few wisps of white cloud. They were some distance from a rocky shore, and Aldar could see other birds spread thinly on the ocean around them; on the rocks, he could see shags and cormorants as well as grey seals gathering in readiness for their own breeding season over the winter months.

He had seen a few of these seals swimming out from the shore and so would frequently duck his head under the surface to ensure none were too close. He and Agata decided this was the day of departure and were about to say their farewells when Aldar saw a sleek grey body immediately below. He ducked his head one more time and saw the seal come to the surface immediately to his seaward side. With a sudden sense of dreadful foreboding, and remembering that this was exactly where Agata sat dozing in the sunlight, he quickly looked up - only in time to see the faintest splash where the animal plunged back beneath the waves. There, where Agata had been just a moment ago, was just a single white feather from her adored belly and the faintest trace of red in the water.

Agata was gone.

29

Puffin Predators

Danger lurks in the sea as well as on land and in the air.

For hundreds of years man was primary predator of Atlantic puffins. Today, although human predation is, thankfully, rare, the human species - through overfishing, pollution of the oceans, discarded plastic, and most of all through climate change - remains the biggest threat to puffins and to all seabirds.

That's not to say, though, that Homo sapiens are the only source of danger. Although they are stocky and tough, puffins are relatively small birds and face predation by foxes, stoats, weasels, cats, and dogs when they are on land. From the air, they are primarily predated by great black-backed gulls and great skuas, although buzzards and other large raptors will also take both adult puffins and chicks. Newly hatched chicks, if they venture from the burrow, may also be taken by smaller gulls such as herring gulls. Puffins are safest, by far, when at sea, although here they may be killed by seals, large fish, or orcas. This is why, when on the surface of the sea, puffins will regularly dip their heads below the surface to check for danger from below. Kleptoparasites (parasitism through the stealing of food) include skuas, herring gulls, and lesser black-backed gulls.

Altogether, life is perilous for the "comics of the sea", but their toughness and adaptability are demonstrated by the relatively high level of survival from one year to the next. This has been estimated at some ninety-five percent survival, unsurprisingly even higher than the estimated rate of survival to adulthood of chicks (some sixty-five percent).

30

Despair

There was no escape from the fog which covered his very existence.

Aldar sat on the now still water, unable quite to take in what had just happened. In one devastating moment, his world had been turned upside down, his future life, as he had expected it to be, rendered void in a fraction of a second. He was stunned into silence and immobility, unable even to consider the danger to himself that might still be present.

The future now seemed to be spread before him, not as one of opportunity and something filled with moments of satisfaction and contented achievement, such as the release of Agneta, but rather as an empty and featureless ocean of despair - a journey into an endless, barren nothingness. He could see no hope, no possibility of escape from the fog that had instantly descended to smother the landscape of his existence.

Unable to think of anything he should do, or anywhere he should go, he simply turned away from the colony, away from the winter he was going to have in the Norwegian Sea, and started to paddle north. He paddled for hour after hour, day after day, without thought, without hope, and without seeing anything around him. Eventually, a gnawing hunger in his belly forced him to dive and feed, but without the usual joy of the hunt, without relishing the taste of food. He simply hunted and ate mechanically, his mind functioning only at the most basic level.

Aldar did not know how many days or weeks passed in this way. The temperature dropped, the days grew shorter, and the nights longer. Storms came and went, winds howled, the ocean moved between a raging tumult and total calm, but nothing - no perception, nothing felt, heard, or sensed - could pierce the world of desolation that surrounded our distraught puffin.

He flew little, simply paddling on and on, always north. Whether he was drawn to something in that direction or whether it was just the way that seemed to take him farthest from the time and place of his grief, he did not know or even care. He just plodded on, living but not alive.

Even when the night sky began to glow with wavering, mercurial light, he did not notice. The phases of the moon waxed and waned, but it meant nothing to Aldar. He paddled, he fed when he was hungry, he drank from the sea when he was thirsty, and none of it had any purpose beyond the moment.

He began to see occasional bluish-white islands of ice float by, always seemingly carried in the direction from which Aldar had come. And still he paddled, or occasionally flew, on northwards. Only when the ice floes began to coalesce into larger islands and block his path did his direction falter. At that point, he just stopped. He still ate and drank and floated on the surface, but his mind lost even this last hint of a goal or direction. So he stopped, and for many days or weeks he simply existed. Without purpose, without hope or desire, without any thought for the future, he simply was.

Until, on a day just like any other, surrounded by an endless sea pocked with jostling white islets of ice, something caught Aldar's eye. A great spout of freezing water erupted into the sky a short distance from him as he sat unthinking and motionless on the surface. The spout was accompanied by a noise of rushing water and a great wind combined into a sound that broke through the background noise of rolling sea and creaking ice. Something stirred in our distraught puffin's mind, some memory from a time before the nothingness, from a time before Agata.

He swam towards where the spout had occurred, and for the second time in his life he saw a great grey mound of living flesh on the surface, bigger than the ice floes all around. The huge mass of this living being drew Aldar towards it like a magnet, as if he were going to merge with it and become just another part of the body itself. As before, those many years ago, Aldar saw the creature's eye and, swimming close, gazed into its depths. Somehow, he recognised that in the mind behind those eyes there was a vast store of experience accumulated through a lifetime which, measured in age or range of travel, was already many times that of the puffin. The creature exuded a calm sense of peace and of acknowledgement and acceptance of the world and its joys and troubles.

There were no words, no exchange of any language, but something of the life force of the whale passed from the centre of its being, through its great, unblinking eye, and into Aldar's small and troubled body. For what seemed like a whole lifetime, Aldar sat in the steady gaze of the whale and absorbed something that triggered a faint and flickering restart of his own life essence. After some time - Aldar had no idea how long - the huge creature broke the connection, moved slowly away from the puffin, and disappeared briefly beneath the waves, only to resurface with a spectacular thrust of its whole body above the surface.

Something of the life force of the whale passed to Aldar in his despair.

It crashed back down onto the surface, sending a wave of cold water that swept Aldar a considerable distance, and when he looked back to where the whale had been, it had gone. With the first deliberate thought for many, many months, our puffin wondered if he would ever see it again. He thought he would, at least once more.

There was no instant reawakening, nor an immediate dispersal of our bird's grief-driven despair, but, over the next days and weeks, he began at last to see with a conscious mind the things around him. He realised he had journeyed far further north than he had ever gone before and began to feel - faintly at first, but growing steadily - the need to return southwards, to return to the living world.

After several more weeks, there came a day when, as he submerged to fish, he recognised a glimmering of satisfaction as he merged movement with his prey, anticipating its next move, before snapping shut his beak at exactly the right place and time to capture it. This catch was a relatively large fish, and Aldar returned to the surface before crunching and devouring his meal. Now, for the first time in he did not know how long, he tasted the meatiness of the fish with a small degree of satisfaction and felt it was something good. The sky was painted with the cascading shimmer of light, which Aldar had been beneath so many times in this winter without seeing - but this time he did see it, and he felt a tiny returning sense of wonder. He saw now how inky black the sky was and how startlingly white, by contrast, was the ice, and just faintly, he recognised a sharper edge to the coldness of the sea and knew that the sea around the colony would be warmer. He turned his head south and felt a small but significant anticipation of the pleasure of the company of other puffins.

He also began to realise that he had, sometime in the passing weeks, moulted last year's drab winter garb, and his attire was now the dapper, sharply delineated colours of summer. He could also see and feel that he had regrown the bright orange and yellow beak decorations with the yellow flower at the corners. In a moment when the sea was suddenly utterly calm, he looked down and saw, reflected back at him, his newly bright face, now as white as the ice with the newly regrown eye decorations of his breeding garb. Suddenly, Aldar felt a wrenching, tearing grief for the passing of Agata - not a repeat of the descent of mind-numbing fog but rather a cathartic bursting of something within. He knew that never again would he see Agata, feel the click of her beak, or hear the gentle growling as she welcomed him back to the nest after a fishing trip. Never again would she surprise him, appearing out of nowhere as he surfaced from a dive in the early spring. He was filled with a sadness he would never lose; however, he also felt the bitter anger he had felt at her loss begin to fade. He knew that, in time, he would remember her with pleasure as the driving force of his early adult years.

But now it was time - time to rejoin the world of living, breathing, growling, stamping, gaping, dancing, nodding, flapping fellow puffins.

Aldar turned south once again.

30

Tangled Again

Aldar struggled, and failed, to contain his rising panic.
Original artwork by Tracy Barnett.

It was many days before Aldar saw any land, and even that was only the far northerly islands. He was in no great hurry, so he mainly paddled on the surface with only a few short flights each day. Of course, he also spent a good deal of time fishing and, achingly slowly, he began to feel the return of the relish of the hunt, as well as his appetite and delight at the taste and texture of his prey. He soon began, occasionally, to see other birds on the sea and in the air and, with some degree of surprise, took pleasure in feeling part of the living world again.

Recovery from his grief was not a linear progression, though. Some days he would return to nearly the stupor of the last winter, but on others there was a steady reawakening of his senses and of his presence amongst other living creatures.

When, finally, he realised he was near to the coast of the colony, the breeding season was well advanced, and Aldar knew it would be too late to find a mate this year. He was not particularly unhappy about this; the wound of Agata's loss was still painfully raw, so he was happy to join the ranks of the unattached hanging around at the edges of puffin society and simply enjoy, for a time, the presence of other puffins.

It did not escape his attention that the burrow he and Agata had painstakingly dug, and which had seen the hatching of several of his offspring, was now occupied by another pair who were busy feeding their own chick. He did not mind this, as he was certain he would never return to that particular nest site but would make a new home when he found a new partner. He spent the long summer days floating on the raft of birds a short distance from the shore, fishing, taking delicious, small, crunchy crabs and shrimp, and nodding amiably to the other birds. This was neither a good year nor a bad one, it would seem; the parents were having to work hard, as the flights to the fishing grounds were long, but not so long that it was impossible to bring sufficient food for the chicks. There were also plenty of fish at the end of the long flights, and so few, if any, chicks would starve this year.

He did notice one change in the colony that puzzled him. The usual continuous din of the kittiwake calls (kittiwaaaaake, kittiwaaake) was not as loud or dense as in previous years. He had also seen several dead kittiwakes floating grotesquely on the sea or cast by the tides onto the rocks below the cliffs, their dead wings flopping languidly as each wave advanced and then retreated. There were gannets among the dead too. Aldar wondered if this was a new type of extermination wrought on the seabirds by humans, who seemed to bring death and destruction with them wherever they went. He feared humans above all predators; they appeared to bring havoc and carnage on a scale that was almost beyond comprehension. Little did he know that he would soon come both to fear humans even more and yet also to be grateful to them.

The season drifted on for Aldar. It was quite something to be in the height of the breeding season and yet not working hard to bring enough food to feed a hungry chick. Not for him, this year, the constant to-and-fro of fishing missions; instead, the year was one of balmy days of socialising and nights of resting on the sea. Aldar was reminded of the first year he had returned to the colony after his juvenile wanderings - those days seemed so long ago, a lifetime past. As the days reached their longest and began to decline, the desire for a long-term partner grew slowly but steadily in Aldar's mind. Next year he would be ready to breed again; there was no puffin alive who could replace Agata, but neither did he want to live out his life as a solitary entity, devoid of any real purpose.

The weather changed, as it always seemed to, after the passing of the solstice, turning wetter and more liable to days of wind and even small storms. The sea grew restless, it seemed to Aldar, wanting to rid itself of all the birds and return once again to its unremarked but relentless pounding of the jagged white cliffs. A few of the earliest arrivals had already fledged their chicks and were preparing to depart again for the winter. The kittiwakes had continued to die in dreadful numbers, and the colony was noticeably quieter in their absence. Their constant calls, usually the dominant sound of the cliffs, were now more evenly matched by the lonely call of the gulls, the grating cough of the fulmars, the mewing of the guillemots, and the almost metallic growling of the razorbills.

Soon Aldar would turn his head north again, but this winter he was not intending to return to the Arctic seas but to the Norwegian Sea, where he had spent his time away from Agata. These intentions, though, were abruptly terminated for our friend on an otherwise nondescript day quite late in the breeding season as he enjoyed his last few days of fellowship with others of his kind.

He had spent the morning bobbing jovially with his fellow puffins in the raft and, as the afternoon wore on, he began to feel a desire for some nice juicy shrimp or a fine pink crab or two. He swam to where he knew there would be a high likelihood of finding such a treat and dove down to the rocky seafloor. In this location, the rocks were enveloped with a whole palette of colours - pink corals, bright red anemones, filamentous green seaweeds, and bright orange starfish. Aldar darted amongst the rocks, looking for the telltale pink shells of his favourite small crabs or the translucent, almost invisible prawns. Seeing the movement of a pink creature in a crevice between two algae-coated rocks, he thrust his head into the gap but missed the crab. He was surprised, on withdrawing, to feel something wrapped loosely around his neck. Unconcerned at first, he made for the surface, thinking it was likely a piece of weed or algae and would fall away as he did so.

Once on the surface, he realised it was still there and attempted to loosen it by shaking his head. This action, though, only made things worse. He realised that something had been trailing behind him and had now wrapped itself around one of his wings. He knew this wasn't one of the great, hanging, filamentous nets of the humans because he hadn't been trapped under the waves but had brought it, whatever it was, with him as he passed from underwater into the open air. He tried to use his powerful feet to pull it free but was even more alarmed when this merely tightened the grip around his neck and immobilised his wing even more.

Aldar struggled and failed to contain the rising panic. He flailed his legs and shook his head, but all that this achieved was to tighten the noose around his neck even further and bind his wing more closely to his body. With a huge effort, he stopped flailing and sat on the water, trying to understand what was happening to him. Every move seemed only to bind him ever more firmly. He managed to take a drink from the ocean but could not move his wing sufficiently to dive beneath the surface, let alone take to the air. Even paddling with his legs served only to tighten the cord, which was so nearly choking him; it was already so tight he could feel it cutting into the back of his neck.

Hours passed agonisingly, and still he had no idea how he could break free. He could feel that he was bleeding, and each tiny move of his body made his situation more desperate. Night came and went, and then another day. He was unable to preen, and even the superbly waterproof feathers of a puffin will eventually become waterlogged if the oils that keep them that way are not replenished. Every breath now was a rasping struggle to draw in enough air. He was drifting in and out of consciousness and was becoming aware that there was no way he could disentangle himself, and so it would seem his life was over. Some part of him hoped that the end would be relatively quick and that he wouldn't suffer the prolonged agony of dying of thirst and hunger. He thought, then, of the abandoned chick and was stabbed by a sharp and dreadful remorse. He thought of Agata and wondered if she hadn't been lucky to have had her life snuffed out so quickly.

By now, he was completely at the mercy of the currents as he could not even paddle his feet without causing searing pain where the cord had sliced his flesh. The current was carrying him towards the shore but also northwards, away from the colony and towards a small bay with a rocky beach backed by steep cliffs. He knew the bay in question and knew it was the haunt of the dreaded humans, but he was completely helpless to do anything to avert being washed ashore there. His only hope was that it was late in the day so that the humans would have departed, leaving him to die in peace.

Finally, the breakers caught him and tumbled him roughly onto the smooth pebbles of the beach. In and out, this way and that, he was dragged helplessly in his semi-conscious state, battered repeatedly against the harsh rocks until he was finally cast higher onto the shore by one particularly large wave. Bedraggled, bloody, bruised, and near death, our long-suffering puffin lay on the rocks and waited for a merciful release.

With what he imagined were his dying thoughts, he remembered his fledged chicks, he thought of Agata, and of the adventures of his youth. He put aside the idea of a renewed partnership and more chicks, and as he passed for the last time into unconsciousness, he saw the great eye of the whale once more and thought of the huge life force of the giant creature, and how a small part had seemed to pass into him in his despair.

And then he thought no more.

31

Other Threats to Atlantic Puffins

The Atlantic puffin, unique and vulnerable.

Atlantic Puffins, along with all North Atlantic seabirds, are subject to a wide range of threats. The status of the species was moved from "least concern" to "vulnerable" in 2018 due to a prolonged and continuing decline in the European population.

Oil:

Puffins are vulnerable to oiling when there are major spills and from routine, if illegal, discharges from shipping. In addition to the immediate impact of the oil, which can cause the bird to drown or die from cold, they will also try to clean the oil from their feathers using their preen gland. This inevitably results in the ingestion of toxic compounds, which can cause inflammation of the stomach and lungs and damage to other organs. Even if the birds survive, this can damage their reproductive success throughout their lives.

Many thousands of puffins are killed by oil every year; some are washed onto the shore, but many more die at sea and are never seen. After the Torrey Canyon disaster in 1967, puffins were only a small proportion of the oiled birds recovered, but in the following years, the number of breeding puffins on the French coast decreased by more than fifteen percent.

Puffins are also vulnerable to other sources of pollution, such as heavy metals. They occupy a high level in the food chain and are therefore likely to experience biogenic concentration of such pollutants in their prey species.

Introduction of Alien Species:

The introduction of predators to puffin breeding colonies is a major risk and can have a devastating impact. On the island of Lundy in the UK, the number of breeding pairs decreased from thousands to just ten by the turn of the millennium, due largely to the presence of rats.

In another example, the island of Craigleith in Scotland has seen a dramatic decline in numbers due to the proliferation of a large species of invasive shrub, the tree mallow, which has dramatically reduced the available land area suitable for puffin burrows.

Hunting:

Historically, hunting has been a major factor in reducing puffin populations, with several instances of overharvesting. As of 2023, hunting is only legal in Iceland and the Faroe Islands, and in both cases, hunting is probably not the major cause of decline; this is rather due to the shortage of prey and climate change.

There are frequent calls for the hunting of puffins to be banned throughout Iceland, but this has not been successful so far.

Climate Change:

The threats from human-induced climate change are widespread and manifold.

Increased storms, particularly in the breeding season, pose a threat. Storms cause direct deaths of puffins but also drive prey fish species into deeper levels of the ocean, beyond the reach of puffins, at a critical time in the reproductive cycle.

The threat from migration of fish species can include both the loss of availability of sand eels and sprats, the most common foods for growing chicks, as well as the introduction of larger fish, such as mackerel, which compete with puffins for food. In addition to these, perhaps more obvious, threats, the introduction to the breeding grounds of new species that replace the usual prey can be devastating. For example, it is evident that changes in the distribution of butterfish, replacing sand eels, is a major contribution to the dramatic decline of puffin numbers in southern Iceland and the Faroes. Butterfish are larger, often too large for the chicks to eat and are also significantly less nutritious.

In the longer term, higher sea levels and increased erosion of coastal cliff areas will exacerbate these threats.

.

32

Humans

The two humans put down their sacks and looked more closely at the puffin.

"Here, Chris, look at this poor puffin."

"It's all wrapped around with fishing net, and it's been bleeding."

"Looks dead, I think, John," Chris replied. "Poor thing. I do wish the bloody fishermen would be more careful where they discard this stuff. It's bloody deadly."

"Aye," said John softly. "Better bag it up, I suppose, so some other creature doesn't try to eat it and get in a similar mess."

John picked up the seemingly dead body of the puffin, but the faintest glimmer of life remained in Aldar, and he reacted to the touch of the dreaded human with the tiniest of shivers.

"Hey, hang on a tick, Chris, it ain't dead," John called to his retreating friend. "It's bloody alive, I tell ya!"

The two humans, on a mission to remove the kittiwake victims of this year's dreadful bird flu epidemic, put down their sacks of inanimate birds and looked more closely at the puffin lying helplessly in John's hands.

"Give it here, John, mate," whispered Chris, and took Aldar from John. Chris was by far the taller of the two friends, at well over six feet tall, but he was something of a gentle giant and held the puffin tenderly in his large hands.

He took out a penknife from his pocket and, adjusting his glasses, tried to cut the plastic thread from around the bird's neck. In doing so, though, he pulled it against the open wound, causing the puffin to shudder with pain. He almost dropped it with the shock of the sharp movement in the bird. It was clearly still alive, even if severely battered, emaciated, and with feathers in a very sorry state.

"Tell you what, Chris, I think I've got a pair of scissors in the first aid kit. Give me a sec," John said urgently.

He unpacked his backpack and found the small but sharp scissors in the kit. He passed them to Chris, who deftly and rapidly snipped the filaments that were cutting into the puffin and then set about removing the rest of the tangle from around its body. He could feel the bird's tiny, rapid heartbeat as he held it tightly in his hands. He didn't want it to panic and hurt itself even more.

"Bloody good job we 'appened along when we did, Chris. I don't think the little blighter would have lasted much longer," said John, peering at the bird now free of the vicious netting. "I'll grab the sacks while you hold on to it, and let's get it up above and see what can be done."

…

Aldar woke in a dazzlingly bright room on the floor of a tiny space covered with bars. He had no memory of being cleaned and given fluids, but he knew he was no longer gripped by the plastic netting. He was no longer struggling to breathe, although his throat hurt and his neck was painfully sore where his flesh had been deeply sliced. He knew also that he was no longer bleeding.

He drifted into unconsciousness again with only a vague thought of what this place was and what new tortures awaited him at the hands of the humans. He assumed it was they who had trapped him and waited until he was washed ashore to capture him.

When he next opened his eyes, he was gripped tightly in the hands of a human female who was prising open his beak and using something to squeeze drops of liquid into his mouth. At first petrified to be captured by one of these dreadful creatures, he soon realised she was not trying to hurt him, and the fluid felt good as he swallowed. She was also murmuring softly, behind something which covered her mouth and nose as she tended him, and her eyes brightened as he opened his. Something told him that this human, at least, was no danger to him, and he let go of the instinct to struggle and try to escape. Once the liquid had all been given to Aldar, she put him back into the container and closed the barred door. Aldar stood on the smooth white floor and looked around.

He was in a small room lit by something on the ceiling. All around him were other boxes just like the one he was in, and some of them contained other creatures, all in some way injured or broken. The whole space smelled of something metallically chemical but not unpleasant. It was not the sea, though, and he couldn't hear the sound of the water that had always been part of his life from the moment he first splashed into it after leaving the burrow. This was the most alien part of this new experience; the sea had always been with him, either around him or beneath him or crashing against the cliffs below the burrow. Here, that constant background noise was absent, no matter how hard Aldar strained to hear it.

He tried to stretch his wings but winced at the tearing pain where the entangling threads had tightened against the left one. Shaking his head was completely out of the question for now. So, in the absence of anything else he could do, Aldar asserted his presence by stamping first with one foot and then with the other. All he could do now was wait to see what fate had in store for him.

He settled down onto the floor of his cage, tenderly tucked his head under his wing, and closed his eyes again.

FISH...

He smelled fish - not alive and succulently fresh, but fish nonetheless. He opened his eyes again and saw that someone, presumably the female human, had placed a container in his cage with half a dozen small sand eels. The smell made him realise he hadn't eaten in days, and he was suddenly aware that he was ravenous. He took a few steps to the container and grabbed one of the fish in his beak, lifted his head, and let it slither down his throat, headfirst. The taste was wonderful, and so was that of the second, and the third, and indeed the rest.

Just as he finished the last one, a part of the wall of the room moved and the human female entered.

"Ah, you're obviously feeling somewhat better," muttered Mary softly to herself. "I think we might have brought you back. You were very close to death when Chris and John brought you in, you know. What a good thing they were still out picking up the poor kittiwakes - I don't think you'd have lasted 'til morning."

Of course, Aldar understood nothing of this, but her voice was gently soothing and inspired trust in her charges. Mary had been doing this a long time and had brought many creatures back from the brink of death, including many other small birds, gulls, gannets, hedgehogs, foxes, and even small seal pups.

"I think we'll try you outside a bit tomorrow, but it'll be a few weeks before we can think of letting you go. Winter's nearly here, and your poor feathers are in a sorry state. They wouldn't keep you dry in an early morning mist, never mind the open sea."

With that, she opened the door to his cage, and Aldar saw she had more fish in her hand. He pecked at them, just as he had pecked at the ones his parents had brought to the burrow a lifetime ago, and, as she let go of them, he caught one in mid-air and swallowed it down. The others fell into the container, and he gobbled the lot.

He saw that another part of his cage held a container of water, and he dipped his beak and drank. As he did so, he watched her bustle around, feeding the other animals or refilling their water containers. Sensing that there was little he could do to alter his situation, Aldar again sat, tucked his head into his wing, and tried to relax. Being in a position where he had no control was somewhat alien to him, but he had been fed, he had water, and he was dry. Although he had a generally battered body and some very nasty cuts, he didn't feel threatened or in immediate peril.

Some time later, the light above him was extinguished, and our puffin presumed that this passed for night in this strange environment. He closed his eyes and slept again, allowing his body to continue to recover. He woke several times during the period of darkness, missing the constant movement of the sea beneath him, until he was finally awakened once more as the light came on again. Unlike the gradual lightening of dawn, this was an immediate transition from dark to bright light, and it seemed to startle all the animals in the room. The female human appeared again and, while making strange musical sounds, which Aldar assumed were the human calls, she proceeded to check each animal, refill water, and present each one with food.

In his turn, Aldar was given more fish. To his taste, these were now stale, and under normal circumstances, he would have left them and hunted for fresher fare. But he thought he had better take what was offered, and so he hungrily ate them all.

Later, the human came to Aldar's cage and, lifting an opening in the top, she reached in to catch hold of him. He moved as far away as he could, but there was nowhere he could go. He pecked at the gloved hand, but this served no purpose, and he was quickly wrapped tightly in the rough material.

"There you go, lovely," Mary said quietly to the bird. "Let's get you into a bigger space and into the open air."

She carried him through the opening which she used to come in and out of the room, and down a long grey passage to where there was an opening through which daylight shone. Passing through into the light, Aldar could see he was now in a space mostly open to the sky, but covered by a mesh of coarse filaments with holes too small for him even to attempt to pass through. The space was completely blue, with a few grey and brown rocks and a tiny "sea" in the centre in which he could see several other birds either paddling or diving - some puffins as well as guillemots and razorbills. Around the edge were several shallow crevices, and in these, again, there were several seabirds. Others stood at the edge of the water or sat with their heads tucked under their wings.

To his horror, Aldar could see that several of the birds had injuries much worse than his, some even with legs missing. One puffin had one of its wings wrapped tightly in some white material, and another had one eye missing. Aldar wondered what horrors had been inflicted on the birds and hoped that nothing of the sort awaited him. Would humans really capture all these birds merely to torture them? The gentle handling and voice of the female human suggested otherwise, but trusting humans did not come naturally to Aldar.

The human carefully lowered him to the floor and let go, and he immediately retreated to the safety of one of the small caves where he looked around to take in this new development. He nodded to other puffins nearby, and one - a young female in what looked like the first incarnation of her breeding plumage - nodded back. Aldar guessed her age at around four years, so she would have been one of those who had spent the year on the edges of the colony but not yet breeding. She didn't appear to have any specific injuries, but her feathers were in dreadful condition and clearly not waterproof.

She smelled somewhat strange too, with a scent unlike any other puffin he had encountered. She had no language to describe what had happened to her, but if she could, she would have told how she had dropped onto the sea one day, only to find there was a nasty, sticky substance floating there that immediately coated her feathers and made flight impossible. She had tried to clean herself, but the substance had a foul taste and burned her throat terribly. She had swum to shore to try to find a safe place where she could try again to clean herself but had only vomited violently before passing into unconsciousness, waking in the same room and in a similar cage to that which had at first contained Aldar.

She woke up held tightly in the hands of the female who was wiping her feathers with a liquid that smelled very strongly of something like flowers. With this liquid, the human was gradually cleaning the oil (which is what it was, although, again, she had no name for it) from her feathers. Eventually, the oil was removed, but this left her feathers totally devoid of her natural oils and completely without waterproofing. She had remained in her cage for several days and had been placed in the blue enclosure just a few days before Aldar arrived.

The two birds nodded again to each other, and Aldar set about sorting his own feathers and using his preen gland to replenish the oil that would render him waterproof once again. The young female did the same, although Aldar could see it would take much longer for her to regain good feather condition; she had lost all her natural waterproofing oils through whatever ordeal she had faced. In this state, even a few minutes on water would leave her waterlogged, cold, and unable to stay afloat or fly.

Aldar worked on his own plumage for several hours before he was satisfied it was sufficiently waterproof. He then ventured to the pool and hopped clumsily in from the side. He looked around to make sure no one, especially the young female he had just met, was judging his entry performance, and then, with a still painful shake of his head, he paddled to the centre and set about giving himself a good wash. He didn't think he would be able to hunt yet, as his flesh wounds were far from healed, and so he was glad when a different human female entered the enclosure and threw in a large amount of fish   not quite the same as freshly caught, as they were already dead, but he admitted it would do. There was a good mix of sprats and sand eels, and there was plenty for all the birds, both those in the pool and those, like the young female puffin, who were still confined to the dry areas.

His hunger satisfied again, Aldar took a stroll around the space, being careful to duck his head as he passed any other puffins who looked like they might decide to be protective of their space. He had little interaction with either the guillemots or the razorbills; the two species were perfectly tolerant of each other, but their lives were entirely separate. This was, as far as Aldar was concerned, exactly how things had always been, should be, and always would be. The other puffins, though, were a different matter. Most remained silent, only using a nod of the head, a short stamping dance, or - in the case of one particularly bad-tempered bird - some beak gaping. This was the correct etiquette when on the water. Some birds, however, were less sure this was the right way, and there were a few low growls, just as there would be in the colony. Most of the birds appeared somewhat confused about where they were and what was going to happen, but all had been through some traumatic event that had led them here, and they were accepting of their current status: being fed and watered and having a pool in which to swim, dive, and clean themselves.

After exploring for some time, Aldar returned to the place where he had first been put and settled onto the floor to nap. The young female was still there, and she too settled down, tucking her legs into her body and her head into her wing.

And so, the pattern of Aldar's life continued as the days grew shorter and the temperature dropped. His wounds slowly healed, and he regained full movement of his head and wings. He was well fed and watered, dry, and warm, but part of him now itched to be away on the open ocean where he would normally be as winter drew on. His female companion had also recovered well and, as she had been able to restore the condition of her plumage, she too had ventured into the pool. Aldar was delighted the first time he was able to dive without pain, and at the next feeding time he spent quite some time pretending the dead fish thrown into the water were alive and needed hunting. Seeing this, the young female followed suit and proved to be an able hunter.

33

Release

Aldar now knew his companion had been Alía.

Towards the end of a day when the sky above the enclosure had been a startlingly bright blue, unsullied by any but the wispiest white clouds, the birds in the enclosure sensed a change. They knew something was about to happen - something new. Two humans entered: one was the gentle-spoken female who had fed and watered them in their initial cages, and the other was a small, gentle-looking man whom only a few of the birds had seen before. The two of them selected a bird - a guillemot - and gently but firmly drove it into a corner before one of them plonked a net over it. They then carefully extracted the bird, placed it in a cage, and took it away. After six fully recovered guillemots had been taken, the two humans next picked out the young female puffin, Aldar's friend. The same process was followed, and she was removed from the enclosure in a cage.

Aldar had a feeling he was next, and so it proved. They cornered him and netted him before placing him in a cage. He wondered what horrors they were going to inflict on him now. Would they remove a leg, as he had seen had happened to some of the other birds, or break a wing so he could no longer fly? Once in the cage, he was taken from the enclosure, back down the long grey corridor, and into the room of the cages. There, they took him out of the cage once more, and while one of them held him firmly, the other pressed a small ring around his leg. It didn't hurt and was so light he could barely feel it, but he also couldn't remove it, as it would not yield to his strong beak.

He was then put back into the cage and carried outside, into the back of one of the moving things that carried the humans around on the land. The others were there, each in its own cage and all looking terrified. Once Aldar had been loaded, the thing moved and the birds were jostled this way and that as it rocked its way to its destination. The journey was not long, and as they came to a stop, Aldar was delighted to smell the sea and hear once again the endless whooshing and crashing of waves against the shore. The doors were opened, enabling him to see that they had stopped halfway down a steep slope that led to a wide bay, surrounded by white cliffs topped with softly sloping, grass-covered soil.

The cages were removed and carried, two at a time, down onto a rocky shore, which Aldar knew was not far from the colony. The sky was still blue but was now beginning to darken towards dusk. The weather was settled, with only a gentle breeze, and the sea, now nearby, lapped gently onto the rocks. Aldar was elated at the proximity of the sea; he could see that all the other birds were similarly excited. Would they actually be released to live their lives again on the wide, ever-changing, ever-moving ocean? Seabirds like Aldar were only truly at home out on the open sea, coming to land only to rear a new chick or to potter briefly at the edge of the colony as other pairs did so. They were creatures of the wind and the waves who only paid brief visits to the land. Aldar's excitement rose at the prospect of returning to his true domain. Was he, after all, going to escape any horrific torture? Was his ordeal really coming to an end?

Two humans were present, and as the large moving box retreated, the birds were left in the company of two male humans, one much taller than the other.

"Right, John, let's get this done, shall we, before it gets dark?" Chris said cheerily. (Aldar knew nothing of the fact that these two were his saviours.) "We'll start with the guillemots and do the two puffins last, shall we?"

"Sounds like a plan," replied John, the shorter of the two.

First, they carried all the cages down the slope and placed them near the edge of the rocks, still a short distance from the water itself. Then, putting the two puffins to one side, they continued chattering away as they gathered all the cages holding the guillemots onto a large flat rock just inches away from the burble of the small wavelets. Once they had all the guillemots together, lined up with one end facing the sea, the two men did something with the end nearest the water, and one by one, they lifted the ends and opened the cages to the air.

For a few seconds, the birds inside didn't know what to do - Aldar had always thought guillemots were a little slow - but first one, then another, and finally the rest made a dash for the open end and threw themselves into the water before paddling rapidly away from the shore. Within minutes, they had all taken to the air and were gone.

The two men watched the guillemots go before turning back towards Aldar and his friend.

"OK, the puffins then," said Chris. "You know, I think I recognise this one. He's lost most of his breeding colours, but I reckon those little jaggedy bits of feather around his neck are where he was so badly cut by the twine of the net. What do you think?"

"Could well be right, Chris. I thought he was a goner for sure, poor little bugger."

"When will we learn that our rubbish kills these things?" asked Chris. "Right, let's do it. I hope they both survive and come back next year to breed."

With that, the two cages were placed on the flat rock in the same way as the other cages had been, and the doors were opened. The two puffins immediately leapt into the sea and paddled a short distance away from the rock. They remained close to each other, and for the first time, they touched and then clicked their beaks together before separating and, running along the sea surface almost parallel, flapping their strong wings to gain flying speed and taking flight almost simultaneously.

The last thing that had passed between them, in whatever way it passed between two puffins, was an exchange of names. Aldar now knew his companion's name was Alía, and she, in turn, knew his.

"Ah, look at that," murmured John. "They're like lovebirds."

"Nah," said Chris more pragmatically, "that male was older, most likely already has a mate who'll be waiting for him next March. She'd be peeved if she thought he was dilly-dallying with a younger bird."

Laughing, the two friends made their way back up the steep slope, away from the chilly but beautiful sea of North Landing, and set off to the nearby pub for a welcome pint.

34

Renewal

Aldar knew he was now ready to make a new life.

Aldar flew for many hours after his release, always heading north and slightly east. He had become used to spending winter in the Norwegian Sea, and this was where he was now headed. He was in good condition after his recuperation, and although it was much later in the year than he would normally have arrived, this presented no problems to a mature bird such as our puffin and he quickly settled into a routine of feeding and riding the Atlantic waves.

The winter was not particularly cold, and although there were several storms, none of these were excessively tumultuous or challenging for a seasoned seabird. Aldar, luckily, suffered few aftereffects from his injuries other than occasional, slight, and fleeting pains at the site of the worst cut on his neck. As Chris had noted, there was a small deformity of the feathers in that region, but this did not adversely affect either the waterproofing of his plumage, nor his swimming or flying ability. Of course, Aldar did not think of any of these things, living mainly in the moment and not dwelling too much on what had gone by or what was to come.

The fishing was neither particularly good nor were fish scarce enough to give a skilled puffin too much difficulty providing for himself. The only lasting effect of Aldar's experience was a reluctance to put his head into any crevice or hole. This rendered a few crabs or shrimps out of reach, but there were plenty of other succulent delights available to him.

So, winter passed, and our bird had survived an adventure that could well have been his last. As spring approached, he again felt the pull of company and the colony, and so he journeyed back, eager to find a new mate and hopefully raise a new puffling. He was ready now; perhaps being so close to death had been the trigger he needed. He would never be able to replace Agata, but he now knew he could make a new life with a new mate.

As usual, on arrival at the colony, he first landed in one of the rafts of birds some distance from shore and took some time to establish his presence amongst the other puffins. He then set out to present himself to the available females. With a shake of his head, he took wing and circled the area widely. There were several gatherings of birds as well as a wider scattering of individuals. As ever, there were those who had already met with their long-term mates, those who were still waiting for their partners to appear, those seeking a new mate, and those not yet ready to breed but returning to the colony for the first time after their juvenile roamings.

Of course, Aldar was now an older, more experienced bird and so a very eligible male, but he was also very choosy. He had seen the worst that a season could throw at a pair and had also reared several pufflings with Agata. She had been a solid and dependable mate, and their bond had been incredibly strong; she would be a hard act to follow.

After some time circling, he spotted what seemed to be a group of singles looking for mates. He put on his best show of landing gracefully (never really successful) near the group, puffed himself up to show off his maturity and strength, and joined them. His beak also showed his greater experience, sporting more ridges than that of a younger bird. Among the group were several older females, presumably having lost partners to some tragedy, although it was possible they had been ousted. Separation or "divorce" was rare in the puffin world but not unheard of; if a partner, male or female, proved inept at raising the cherished chick or poor at providing fish, they could indeed be replaced. These didn't carry placards, of course, so the selection process was not entirely straightforward.

Aldar had not yet seen anyone who created an instant attraction, nor, it must be said, had his charms enticed any ardent prospects. He paddled a little way from the group, intending to hunt, when he became aware of a young female alongside him. Her scent seemed familiar, as did the way she held herself. Her new breeding plumage was worn with a mix of demureness and the confidence of youth, typical of a bird new to breeding. She looked strong, robust, and healthy. But what was it about her that seemed so familiar?

She was looking closely at Aldar, tilting her head this way and that as if to place him in the right position in her gaze. Suddenly, and simultaneously, it clicked for both of them - this was Alía, Aldar's friend from the recovery centre. At the time, he had not considered her as a mate, and nor had she looked at him in that way; they had merely been thrown together by circumstance. Although they had grown quite close during their stay, there had been nothing more between them at that time, as neither had been looking for a mate.

She looked closely at Aldar, tilting her head this way and that.

Now, though, they were both looking for a mate among the unattached puffins. Each contemplated the other for some time, as if considering whether the change from friends to partners was something they wanted. In the end, it was Alía who made the first move. She paddled close to Aldar and gingerly extended her brightly coloured bill in his direction. After only a fleeting moment, he responded, and their beaks touched lightly. Swimming together now, they moved their beaks in unison and began the clicking that would cement their bond. The decision was made; it would seem that the bond of friendship was now to be deepened into that of lifelong breeding partners. From this moment, they would find each other every spring, and after mating, would raise their single puffling before separating again for the winter months.

The two partners continued to bond for some time on the water. They clicked beaks, hunted together, and sat quietly in the fading sunlight, content in each other's company. The sun dipped behind the hills of the land in front of them, and with its last rays for the day, it washed the clouds with brilliant yellows, fading first to orange and then to deep red before the colour bled from them and they returned to grey against a pale but darkening sky.

With morning, the two birds, already mated, set about finding their new burrow. Aldar's experienced eye, along with a dominance that came with age and maturity, helped them secure a prime position near the centre of the colony, where they could dig in the soft earth above the cliffs to create their new home. In a reprise of his first nest-building many years ago, he did most of the digging, several times covering Alía with loose earth as she stood at the entrance to the deepening hole. She cleared away the loosened earth to ensure the burrow was fronted by a space where they could land after fishing and also stand together to cement their partnership and display their ownership to their neighbours.

The digging continued for several weeks, while the two continued to cement their new partnership and mate frequently. The final two digging tasks were the widening of the nest chamber itself and the creation of a side chamber where the chick, once hatched, could defecate so keeping the main burrow clean. Once all of this was complete, the two partners could be seen gathering sticks, moss, grass, feathers, and other materials - not all of them suitable for nest building, it must be said, with Alía in particular showing a penchant for bringing in stones. All was complete in time for her to lay her first egg, and she and Aldar stood admiring it for some time. It was white, with just a little light brown mottling, pointed at one end and broad at the other, and a good size. Alía thought she had done well to grow and then lay an object of such size.

Both parents had developed bald patches on their bellies, which allowed them to bring their skin into direct contact with the egg during brooding, providing warmth to progress the incubation process. As always, Aldar took the first shift, allowing Alía to go and feed. For the next forty days or so, there would usually be one or other of them sitting on the egg. Only occasionally, on a particularly balmy evening, might both be found standing at the burrow entrance for a short time, exchanging greetings with their neighbours and parading up and down on their short landing strip to display their ownership. Only once had another puffin challenged Aldar at the entrance, hoping to take over the burrow. Aldar had seen the challenger off with a bout of wrestling that sent both of them tumbling down the cliff, leaving the other in no doubt whatsoever of Aldar's dominance, strength, and maturity.

And so, in time, the egg hatched, revealing an initially wet, bedraggled, and sticky puffling. But this ungainly being soon dried and fluffed up as the two adults continued to keep it warm for the first week, alternating sitting and fishing between them. Once the puffling was able to maintain its own temperature, the parents set about the task of fetching enough food to keep their offspring growing. The season was a tough one, as the main fish stocks seemed once more to have migrated some distance from the colony and were not plentiful. Aldar's several years of experience proved invaluable as he was able to guide Alía to the best fishing spots and show her how to avoid the predations of the marauding gulls. He usually managed to return with a very full beak, supplementing Alía's endeavours in this, her first rearing season. He was adept at scooping up prey once found, lining them up in the grooves on his beak and keeping them in place with the serrations of his upper mouth and a strong tongue. Together with Alía's youthful energy and dedication, the pair our partners proved able parents, and despite the difficulties, the puffling matured in good time.

On the momentous day when, in Aldar's judgement, she was ready to fledge, the weather was calm, if wet. A constant rain had fallen for days, and there had even been some small landslips, although none affecting our pair's burrow. The landing and launching strip was a little slippery though and this probably contributed to the speed with which the new fledgling launched herself on her first flight - perhaps a mix of a conscious decision to go and a slip-slide off the edge. Either way, she successfully made the safety of the sea and by morning had gone far into the open water, bearing her newly given name of Anelía.

Our proud and successful parents spent the customary few days enjoying each other's company after the strains of rearing their chick - a time they used to rekindle their bond before both departed to spend the winter in their own favourite ranges. Aldar reflected on the season and on the ups and downs of his life. Would Agata have approved of his new mate, he wondered? He would never know the answer, but he did know that he was as committed to this partnership as he had been to Agata. He hoped this one would not end so tragically.

35

Encounter Three

The years began to weigh heavily on Aldar.

The years continued, with winter spent alone and spring and summer dedicated to rearing more pufflings: Angelika and Aníta, Aðalríkur and Arnór, and more. There were hard years, and even two more lost chicks - one taken by a large black-backed gull that swooped down unseen as the chick emerged too early one evening, and one lost again to a shortage of food. The fish in that year were strange, a different species that didn't seem to have the nutritional value of the sandeels, leading to a large proportion of pairs failing to raise chicks.

The kittiwakes slowly recovered their numbers, and the populations of puffins, guillemots, and razorbills waxed and waned with the years. Every year, spring seemed to arrive earlier, and with it the maximum population of prey. The puffins struggled to adapt their breeding to this shift, as well as to the continual effects of higher temperatures, which increased the frequency and severity of storms. These storms seemed to grow more intense and more frequent with every passing year, sometimes storms historically more likely to be found in winter would pound the shores throughout the breeding season. Each of these things combined to make the rearing of chicks ever more difficult, combined, of course, with the increasing age, particularly of Aldar.

One year, something like their fifteenth as a pair, Alía's egg simply didn't hatch, and the following year she did not return from the winter. Aldar knew she had reached the end of her life. He was sad, but without the devastation he had felt at the loss of Agata, who had been so young. For two seasons more Aldar returned to the colony as an onlooker only, too old now to attract a partner and, if he was honest with himself, without any interest in doing so. His breeding suit of white facial plumage, bright beak and legs, and yellow, wrinkled rosette still appeared, but much duller now, reflecting his declining ability to hunt and feed during the winter.

At the beginning of the fourth winter after Alía failed to return, and following a particularly mellow autumn, Aldar felt a growing compulsion to return once again to the far north. Battling through some particularly fierce storms that reminded him of his first winter, through constant rain and occasional snow, he plodded slowly on his way, feeding little in those days, just sufficient to maintain his strength for the journey. He passed the latitudes of the islands where he had once been hunted by humans and pondered on that strange species, seemingly so intent on doing harm. He remembered, also, though the ones he had met in the rescue centre who had nursed he and Alía back to health and then released them back to the sea. Humans, he decided, were not all bad but were still to be feared, especially in groups. Much of the havoc they wreaked seemed to be without specific intent, simply the result of a careless and utterly casual relationship with the world. Whatever they wanted, they would take without any thought to the consequences for other species or for the future. When this was coupled with their obvious power over nature, they were a formidable threat not just to puffins but to all species.

If Aldar could have experienced human society, he would have known that there were many humans who agreed with him and tried to change and improve the way humans used the planet's resources. Sadly, they were outnumbered by those who never gave such things a thought, caring only for their own immediate gratification.

And so, with these sanguine thoughts, Aldar continued his journey. He had no memory of much of his first exploration further north, than his current location as at that time he had been functioning almost entirely on auto-pilot, with little recognition of his surroundings. This time, he was able to note the gradual decrease in the temperature of the sea and the change in prey species. The days were also shortening rapidly, and on one moonless night, he saw, again, the sky painted with ever-shifting blue, green, yellow, and orange lights. He realised he had come as far north as he had on that first journey, although, apart from a very few small and flimsy floating islets, there was no sign of significant ice. Aldar wondered at this and suspected that it too was caused by the ravening humans. Was there no end to their depredations, he thought to himself.

He now knew he simply needed to wait, and so he spent his days fishing and preening, maintaining his position facing into the cold winds of the north. Again and again, he watched the skies and their reflections in the sea come alight with the bright and mysterious lights. He watched the sun sink lower and lower in the sky until, one day, it did not rise above the horizon. All that existed now was the deep dark of night and a brief, shadowy twilight. By this time, he was very weary and would spend large amounts of time simply sleeping on the surface of the sea, waking only to drink or, occasionally, to conduct a half-hearted hunt for fish. The days continued in this way for a few weeks until, finally, after a particularly cold spell that had littered the sea once again with ice, Aldar knew the day he had been waiting for had arrived.

He first became aware of a high-pitched glooping, trilling, a high clicking song in the depths of the ocean. He hadn't been fully conscious of it in his previous encounters, but now he realised its significance and watched keenly for the next sign. Soon enough, he saw the great spout of water that signalled the arrival of the whale. Aldar forced his weary body into motion and paddled to reach the place where it had occurred.

He arrived to see the great body of the humpback whale lying on the surface and could feel again the great breaths the animal took as it replenished its oxygen supply before it would dive more deeply than Aldar had ever dreamt possible. Once more, he saw the great orb of the whale's eye and swam towards it. He felt clearly that the beast recognised him and perhaps also recognised the loan of life force it had given him to bring him back from his depths of despair. The two beings, one tiny and relatively fragile, the other huge and seemingly impervious to harm, sat alongside each other, somehow sharing the significance of their common, if also very disparate, place in the network of the life of the world.

Aldar felt himself drawn closer and closer to the eye and seemed to be seeing - indeed, he imagined himself swimming - deep into the depths of the whale's being. The two maintained that position for some time, and then the whale tucked its great head beneath the waves, once more raised its fabulous tail and brought it down onto the sea with a tumultuous crash as if in a final salute of his friend. Then it passed slowly beneath the waves. The surface of the sea it left behind was eerily calm, reflecting with dazzling precision the bright stars above. The inert body of a small puffin drifted slowly away with the current.

The End

References

In making this book I have used many sources to gain information on Puffin lives and natural history. I am grateful to all the following:

Bloomsbury Wildlife - https://acbwildlife.wordpress.com/

International Council for Bird Preservation – The Danger of Gill Netting to Seabirds, Natasha Atkins and Burr Henemen

Effects of Gill-Net Fishing on Marine Birds in a Biological Hotspot in the Northwest Atlantic – Gail K. Davoren (Conservation Biology Vol. 21, No. 4 (Aug., 2007)

https://environment.ec.europa.eu/topics/nature-and-biodiversity/natura-2000_en

https://www.birdguides.com/articles/migration/young-puffins-work-out-their-own-migration-routes

https://app.bto.org/ring/countyrec/resultsall/rec6540all.htm

https://puffinsandclimatechange.weebly.com/the-future-for-atlantic-puffins.html

A Dispersive Migration in the Atlantic Puffin and Its Implications for Migratory Navigation (Tim Guilford, Robin Freeman, Dave Boyle, Ben Dean, Holly Kirk, Richard Phillips, Chris Perrins - https://journals.plos.org/plosone/article?id=10.1371/journal.pone.0021336)

https://www.natgeokids.com/uk/discover/animals/birds/puffin-facts/

https://www.nationalgeographic.com/science/article/140827-seabird-puffin-tern-iceland-ocean-climate-change-science-winged-warning

The Secret Lives of Puffins – Dominic Couzens and Mark Sisson

https://www.seabird.org/threats

https://en.wikipedia.org/wiki/Project_Puffin

https://en.wikipedia.org/wiki/Atlantic_puffin#Description

https://rias-aldeia.blogspot.com/2023/06/primeiro-papagaio-do-mar-recuperado.html

https://www.portugalresident.com/rias-nurses-its-first-atlantic-puffin-back-to-health/

https://en.wikipedia.org/wiki/Atlantic_puffin

https://www.johnmooremuseum.org/the-buzzard-buteo-buteo/

Hinterland Whos Who – Atlantic Puffin https://www.hww.ca/en/wildlife/birds/atlantic-puffin.html#:~:text=The%20main%20predators%20of%20puffins,not%20a%20threat%20to%20adults.

https://www.hww.ca/assets/pdfs/factsheets/atlantic-puffin-en.pdf

https://www.nordicnames.de/wiki/Icelandic_Names

https://www.cbc.ca/news/canada/new-brunswick/atlantic-puffin-rescue-pam-novak-wildlife-institute-riverview-1.6770582

The dynamics of gull-puffin interactions: implications for management Suzanne K. Finney - https://core.ac.uk/download/pdf/293042151.pdf

The diet of Atlantic Puffin Fratercula arctica and Northern Gannet Sula bassana chicks at a Shetland colony during a period of changing prey availability A.R. Martin

https://www.allaboutbirds.org/guide/Atlantic_Puffin/overview

https://www.nationalgeographic.com/travel/article/norways-best-kept-secret-puffin-dogs

https://marinescotland.atkinsgeospatial.com/nmpi/default.aspx?layers=478

https://www.rspb.org.uk/

https://www.worldwildlife.org/blogs/good-nature-travel/posts/ten-high-flying-facts-about-puffins#:~:text=3.,2.

Puffins on Skomer Island, Wales Ruth E. Ashcroft Ornis Scandinavica (Scandinavian Journal of Ornithology) Vol. 10, No. 1 (1979)

https://www.birdforum.net/gallery/puffin.705706/

https://birdfact.com/articles/baby-puffins

Peter Corkhill (1973) Food and Feeding Ecology of Puffins, Bird Study, 20:3, 207-220, DOI: 10.1080/00063657309476382 https://doi.org/10.1080/00063657309476382

The Puffin Book – Drew Buckley

Adult survival rates for Atlantic puffins:-

https://www.researchgate.net/publication/232686476_Adult_survival_rates_of_Atlantic_Puffin_Fratercula_arctica_at_two_colonies_in_the_Gulf_of_Maine

I am sure there are many other sources which I have referred to over the years to increase my knowledge of puffins. I apologise if I have missed any from here.

www.ingramcontent.com/pod-product-compliance
Lightning Source LLC
Chambersburg PA
CBHW041307020426
42333CB00001B/6